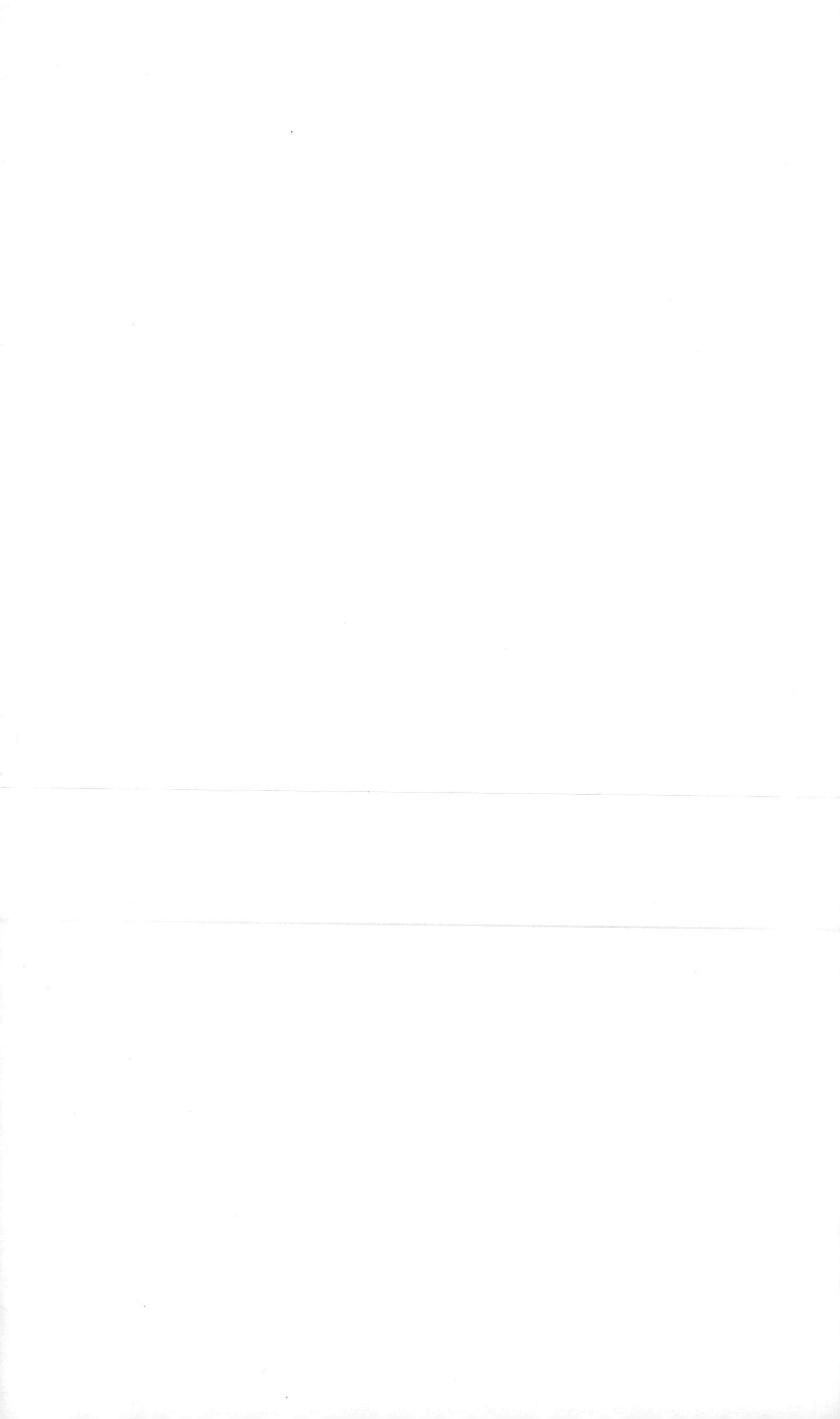

LIGHT OF LIBERTY

LIGHT OF LIBERTY

JUSTIN NICHOLSON

DONNIE SWAGGART

Illustrations by Jonathan Snowden

JIMMY SWAGGART MINISTRIES
P.O. Box 262550 | Baton Rouge, Louisiana 70826-2550
www.jsm.org

ISBN 978-1-941403-37-2

17 18 19 20 21 22 23 24 25 26 / EBM / 10 9 8 7 6 5 4 3 2 1

TABLE OF CONTENTS

FOREWORD

"Where there is no religion, there is no morality. With the loss of religion, the ultimate foundation of confidence is blown up; and the security of life, liberty, and property are buried in ruins." – Timothy Dwight, president of Yale College, 1795-1817

As many of you know, I am a lover of history. Though not a scholar, I am an ardent student of our past. This book was written for one reason, and one reason alone. Our nation no longer knows its own history. Godless professors teaching in our universities have become purveyors of fake history. They try to say that our nation was founded as a secular endeavor. Now we get to prove them wrong.

Noah Webster once said, "The moral principles and precepts contained in the Scriptures ought to form the basis of all our civil constitutions and laws. All the miseries and evils which men suffer from, vice, crime, ambition, injustice, oppression, slavery, and war, proceed from their despising or neglecting the precepts contained in the Bible."

Now, you, the reader, will have the truth at your fingertips

—the words, the letters, and the speeches. All we have to do is let our Founding Fathers speak for themselves in their own words.

Benjamin Rush said, "The only foundation for a useful education in a republic is to be laid in religion. Without this there can be no virtue, and without virtue there can be no liberty, and liberty is the object and life of all republican governments." Rush added, "Without religion, I believe that learning does real mischief to the morals and principles of mankind."

This book is not meant to be a complete study of our forefathers or of America's history in general, but, instead, it is the first step for those who want to know more about its *true* history. My prayer is that this book will spur you to dig deeper and further educate yourself on the countless people who shaped America's history and the influence of Christianity in their lives. This is their story.

— Donnie Swaggart

PREFACE

When I received my creative writing degree from Louisiana State University in 2007, I never imagined that I would write a book that actually meant something.

I chose creative writing because I loved to write, but I never took my writing very seriously. I was the funny guy. Sketch comedy and silly short stories, that was my game. Young, naive, and fresh out of college, I envisioned myself taking the comedy world by storm—packing my bags for New York and writing for *Saturday Night Live*. But, it was not to be. The Lord, instead, guided me to SonLife Broadcasting Network (SBN).

Fast forward to March 2017, and I am sitting here in my office at SBN, putting the finishing touches on this book. I never imagined that I had the qualifications to write this book, yet, throughout the course of researching, writing, and countless hours of rewriting, it became clear that this project was devised by God for such a time as this.

When this project was brought to me, we were in the midst of production on our first season of *Preachers, Patriots, & Providence*. The fact is, when you're limited to one hour per episode on television, you're also limited to the amount of information that you can pack into each episode. But, Brother Donnie had a vision. He came up with the idea for a companion book to the series—a book that would expand on the success of the television program and deliver an even greater wealth of information to a hungry audience. That is what you hold in your hands today. It was my job to bring Brother Donnie's vision to light.

I would like to thank the Swaggart family for entrusting me with this endeavor. It was challenging at times, but without their belief in me, I never would have believed in myself. I would also like to thank Jonathan Simmons who stood by my side every step of the way throughout this journey. I could not have done this without him. The same goes for Hazel Semper, Dave Cooper, Matthew Simmons, Caleb Berg, Amy Duplessis, and countless others in my SBN family who had a hand in this book.

Light of Liberty is a journey. It's a journey of discovery, a journey of truth, and a journey of America's identity. It is the true story of Christianity's role in the founding of the United States of America.

Men and women from all walks of life dreamed of establishing a nation—a free nation; a nation based on biblical principles; a nation solely guided by God's will; and a nation everstanding under His protection. Most of these men and women never understood what they were about to achieve or the legacy they would leave behind. But, leaving a legacy was the furthest thing from their minds. For them, it wasn't a certainty; it was a calling.

Some called it a grand experiment, but, in reality, it would be the ultimate testament to a nation's calling—a calling defended by the Word of God and acknowledged by the providence of God.

And now, we get to tell their story.

—Justin Nicholson

Martin Luther walks to Castle Church to nail his Ninety-Five Theses.

CHAPTER 1

LET THERE BE LIGHT

CHAPTER ONE
LET THERE BE LIGHT

Is the United States of America a Christian nation?

Those who have studied the founding of the United States of America often call to remembrance the Founding Fathers, but often overlooked are the contributions that a number of other key patriots provided to the colonists. Among these American patriots were some of the most powerful preachers the world had ever seen. But, just because someone was considered a patriot or a Founding Father, it doesn't mean he was Christian. Men like Thomas Jefferson, Benjamin Franklin, and Thomas Paine, who were pivotal to the charge of independence, were not necessarily Christians, but they were still guided by God's will in establishing a nation under His protection. But, as important as understanding the men and women who dared to defy the British Empire, they were nothing without the providence of God and the power unleashed by the Word of God.

"In the beginning God created the heaven and the earth." (Gen. 1:1).

Everything has a beginning. The very first verse of the Bible tells us that. Therefore, if we're going to adequately answer the question, "Is the United States of America a Christian nation?" we have to trace the roots of Christianity all the way back to 16TH century Europe at the dawning of a new era in Christendom—the Protestant Reformation.

The development of a new Christian discourse of faith would produce a new religious theology and philosophy within Christianity. Reformation theology would not only open an expanding discussion concerning spiritual understanding and authority, but it would also lead to decades of strife and conflict, changing the course of history. The Reformation pulled the world out of the Dark Ages and into a new era, so why would it cause such a stir in 16TH century Europe? Because it was a message of joyful certainty in an age of uncertainty.

In a land drowning in a sea of gloom and corruption, a dynasty of theological darkness held humanity captive. This land: the Holy Roman Empire. Its captors: the Roman Catholic Church. At the head of this dynasty was the pope. Within this dynasty was an army of followers who held the authority of the papal office above all else. In order to combat this evil scourge of power, it would take an opposing army of men—men like John Wycliffe and Martin Luther—men who felt a significant calling to take a stand against the authority of the church. These courageous attempts to follow their hearts and spread the truth of the gospel would change the face of Western civilization.

At the time of the Middle Ages, the landscape of the Holy Roman Empire lay in a deep pool of impurity and filth. The concept of sanitation was something to be desired. Livestock dwelled under the same roof as their peasant owners, and pungent odors permeated the air. The fragility of human life was all too dire. Man faced a number of obstacles, crippling diseases, and various uncertainties (wars, famine, plague), yet, this all paled in comparison to the greatest uncertainty of them all: the uncertainty of eternal life.

The church had drifted into a state of apostasy. For centuries, a dark cloud loomed overhead. The papacy withheld the Bible from the common people's hands; therefore, very few souls were actually saved. The door to the gospel was locked, and Satan held the key. He found great success in generating and maintaining the uncertainties of life. It was this bondage that chained mankind to the shackles of sinful darkness.

The Roman Catholic Church reigned supreme—not just theologically and politically, but economically, as well. Priests were assigned to every village to oversee the daily activities of life from the church to the common market, from the schools to civil affairs.

The Catholic Church thrived under the concept of "canon law." According to canon law, the pope was the ultimate authority on earth. The Word of God was disregarded. This gross abuse of power allowed the pope to control nearly every aspect of life. As corruption emanated from Rome, godly men began to stir and became increasingly outraged. A storm was brewing.

While many experts consider Martin Luther to be the pivotal agent for sparking the Reformation, it was Englishman John Wycliffe who, two centuries before, began to spark a revolution. He was the crucial first step in this greater movement—that step being the first translation of the Bible into the English language, finally making the literal words of God available to the masses.

Wycliffe was renowned for his intellectual capacity. In 1372, after years of intensive education, Wycliffe received his doctorate of theology from the University of Oxford. Wycliffe became increasingly aware of the Catholic Church's abuse of power, turning him into a staunch dissident of their doctrines.

He became disillusioned with the overall embodiment of the church, arguing that the Bible should be the authoritative center of Christianity—not a system of laws and traditions established by the pope. Wycliffe denounced the deceptive works of priests, specifically the sale of indulgences.

> It is plain to me that our prelates in granting indulgences do commonly blaspheme the wisdom of God. —John Wycliffe

Under canon law, priests diligently pushed the sale of indulgences—a payment for the remission of one's sins with a small financial sacrifice. From the crowds of purchasers to the shouts of the sellers, it looked much like a market, but a market conducted by monks. The merchandise they were selling, at which they offered a reduced price, was the salvation of souls.

The common criminal was led to believe that he could do whatever he wanted and then acquire an indulgence to receive forgiveness for his sins, in effect, fending off time in purgatory and gaining entry into the portals of heaven, with the Catholic Church acting as mediator before God. This bizarre practice flourished all throughout the European landscape, enraging Wycliffe.

He exhorted his fellow ministers to preach the gospel, not fables or entertainment, so that those with attentive, spiritually hungry minds would be grounded by faith in one biblically-centered gospel.

Wycliffe believed the Bible should be consumed on a daily basis, not just by the religious elite, but also by the multitudes. He thoroughly read through the Scriptures, interpreting them and applying them to his own life. The revelation of these Scriptures opened Wycliffe's eyes, enabling him to see the nefarious system of the Catholic Church and its opposition to the Word of God.

Speaking out against the pope's possession of total political and social control, Wycliffe believed that the church should limit itself to its own jurisdiction. The church's primary affairs should be of the spiritual realm, not political. Thus, Wycliffe became one of the first men to promote the separation of church and state.

He contended that the Catholic Church was deep in transgression. In fact, Wycliffe declared the entire embodiment of the Catholic Church a misguided and corrupt practice of religion.

One example of that corruption was the papal schism, in which three different men simultaneously claimed to be the vicar of Christ.

A resolution was reached, unifying the church under one pope, but many eyes were awakened to the perversion of government within the Catholic Church. The damage done to its reputation was irreparable, further confirming Wycliffe's declarations.

With such bold declarations, Wycliffe quickly garnered a following. Through earnest teaching, eloquent preaching, and his unbending courage, he won the esteem and confidence of his peers.

The more clearly Wycliffe discerned the errors of the papacy, the more fervently he presented the teaching of the Bible. He saw that Rome had forsaken the Word of God for human tradition, and he fearlessly accused the priesthood of having abandoned the Scriptures. Wycliffe demanded that the Bible be restored to the people and that it be established once again as the sole authority of the church.

As Wycliffe's ideas spread, Rome took notice. Church authorities were filled with furor when they perceived that this dissident was gaining influence.

In 1377, Wycliffe was summoned to appear before a group of bishops at St. Paul's Church in London to answer to charges of heresy. He was escorted by two of his most powerful supporters—Lord Percy, the marshal of England, and John of Gaunt, the head of the English government.

Tempers flared and threats clamored at Wycliffe's entourage as they made their way through the crowds to the front doors of St. Paul's Church. Wycliffe had a striking appearance about him, replete with dignity and character. He was confident and not to be intimidated.

> I am ready to defend my convictions even unto death.
> —John Wycliffe

At the onset of the proceedings, John of Gaunt told Wycliffe he could sit rather than stand. The bishops were enraged at the gall of this gesture. The two parties exchanged a barrage of insults. John of Gaunt even threatened to drag one of the bishops from the cathedral by the hair on his head. No longer than it took for the meeting to begin, onlookers siding with the church revolted against Wycliffe and his companions. The scene became so chaotic that Wycliffe and his party were forced to flee for their lives.

Wycliffe knew that if the true gospel of Christ were to ever gain a greater influence on the hearts of the common people, the Bible would have to be translated into their language. During the Middle Ages, there were no Bibles in the common tongue. If one were to get his hands on a Bible, it was written in Latin, and only skilled or highly educated men could read it. The common people were left to the mystic, pagan views of the village priests, many of whom had never read the Bible themselves. In 1380, Wycliffe and other trusted colleagues began work on the very first English translation of the Bible.

The church bitterly opposed it: "By this translation, the Scriptures have become vulgar, and they are more available to lay, and even to women who can read, than they were to learned scholars, who have a high intelligence. So the pearl of the gospel is scattered and trodden underfoot by swine."

Wycliffe replied, "Englishmen learn Christ's law best in English. Moses heard God's law in his own tongue; so did Christ's apostles."

John Wycliffe escaped martyrdom and died of a stroke on December 31, 1384, but the revolution he launched did not follow him to the grave. His teachings, though suppressed, only prospered after his death, thanks to his followers, known as the "Lollards"—a term that was considered derogatory at the time and referred to those with little to no academic understanding. They were also quite possibly the first known Protestant group of that era to ever walk the earth. The Lollards continued to preach the gospel, in spite of death threats from the English Parliament. They believed in the authority of the Scriptures, placing the utmost importance in a personal relationship with Jesus Christ through faith. All in all, the Lollard movement made a significant impact on England.

The Catholic Church convicted John Wycliffe of more than 250 charges of heresy on May 4, 1415—more than 30 years after his death. They banned his writings and subsequently burned all of his works. To add insult to injury, Pope Martin V issued an order for a posthumous execution. John Wycliffe's remains were dug up and burned, with his ashes being cast into the river Swift. But, ironically, and perhaps symbolically, his ashes traveled down the river Swift, where it met a number of smaller streams that emptied into the waters of the great Atlantic, spreading his influence—literally—all over the world.

As a later chronicler observed, "Thus the brook hath conveyed his ashes into Avon; Avon into Severn; Severn into the narrow seas; and they into the main ocean. And, thus, the ashes of Wycliffe are the emblem of his doctrine, which now is dispersed the world over."

It is no wonder that Wycliffe has been widely characterized as the "morning star" of the Reformation. He was a reformer before the Reformation. For him, the Bible was not just one authority among several others. It stood above all.

> Trust wholly in Christ. Rely altogether on His sufferings; beware of seeking to be justified in any other way than by His righteousness. Faith in our Lord Jesus Christ is sufficient for salvation. There must be atonement made for sin according to the righteousness of God. The person to make this atonement must be God and man. —John Wycliffe

Wycliffe died a reformer, who never felt himself to be a heretic, but only a preacher whose utmost desire was to see the church cleansed of its unrighteousness and obedient to the Lord.

John 4:37 says, *"And herein is that saying true, One soweth, and another reapeth."* Wycliffe's life embodied that Scripture in that where one sows, another waters, and yet another reaps the harvest. From his efforts, Wycliffe would not reap the harvest, but God was grooming another man— a man who would not cower, a man who would not yield, a man who dared to stand against the stronghold of Rome and bring about a divine change in Christianity.

> To gather with God's people in united adoration of the Father is as necessary to the Christian life as prayer. —Martin Luther

On November 10, 1483, Martin Luther was born to Hans and Margaretta Luder in the small town of Eisleben, Germany. Having been born into the Holy Roman Empire, Luther was immediately ushered into the strict Catholic lifestyle.

Martin Luther's father, owning a nearby copper mine, saw his profession as harsh and often dangerous. He aspired for his son to ascend to a greater calling. He sent a young Martin Luther away to a highly regarded school. At the age of 17, he entered the University of Erfurt, a premiere university in Germany, where he received his bachelor's degree in only two years and his master's by the age of 22. Obeying his father's wishes, young Luther went on to study law.

Luther became increasingly drawn to theology and philosophy. He was determined to seek out the meaning of life through these avenues, but he soon found little satisfaction in the ideals of philosophy. His concentrated studies made him aware of the need for divine intervention, spiritual truth, and salvation, but this did not mean he understood the true grace of God. In reality, Luther was attempting to be righteous in God's sight through works. Martin Luther became increasingly eager for a change in his life that would fill the void in his heart.

Martin Luther had been attending law school for only a few weeks when his father sent for him to come home and celebrate his recent graduation from the university. On his journey home, Luther found himself in the midst of a tumultuous thunderstorm. The night sky lit up in a magnificent display of nature. The rains poured. The thunder crashed. Suddenly, a lightning bolt struck near him. Stricken with panic, terrified, and desperate, he cried for help: "Help, St. Anne! I'll become a monk!" In times of great adversity, a true believer knows to call on the name of Jesus, but for Martin Luther, he knew no better.

After this declaration, the storm quickly subsided, and Luther emerged unscathed. To him, a bolt of lightning was a sure sign of God's judgment. Having been spared of his life and seeing this as divine intervention, Luther kept his bargain with St. Anne, dropped out of law school, and immediately entered an Augustinian monastery, much to the chagrin of his father. His joining of this religious order began a journey that would lead him from a confused, young monk to a man who would defy an empire.

Feeling haunted by the insecurity of his salvation, he felt the monastery to be a perfect venue to seek assurance. Life as a monk was not simple, and Luther did not haphazardly undertake his devotion to the boundaries of monkhood. Every waking minute was dedicated to rigorous amounts of fasting, prayer, confession, and pilgrimages—even flagellation.

His room was small. It contained one chair, a candlestick, and a straw bed. There was no heating, which made the winters nearly unbearable. He would beg for food in the streets, not for economic reasons, but for spiritual humility. Eating only once a day, he became brutally thin, practically flesh and bones. His fragile, bony figure was distinctly visible through his gown.

Yet, after all of this self-inflicted torment, peace with God escaped him. The more he tried to do for God, the more he became aware of his sinfulness. Nothing he did could suppress his spiritual turmoil. The assurance he so longed for evaded him.

Luther would later describe this part of his life as one of great spiritual despair. "I lost touch with Christ the Saviour and Comforter, and made of him the jailer and hangman of my poor soul."

He found limited encouragement in Johann von Staupitz, vicar general of Luther's monastery. Staupitz decided that Luther needed more work to distract him from constantly mulling over himself. He ordered Luther to pursue an academic career, and in 1507, Luther was ordained into the priesthood.

Three years later, Luther was given the opportunity to be a delegate to a church conference in Rome. Staupitz believed this trek to Rome would revitalize Luther's devotion, not only to God but, also, to the Catholic Church.

Upon Luther's arrival in Rome, he witnessed nothing less than a hotbed of debauchery. There was witchcraft in the streets, luxury and apathy among his fellow clergymen, priests soliciting prostitutes, and ignorant clerics with no compassion for the spiritually broken. He became more disillusioned than ever. Discouraged by the immorality, wickedness, and corruption he witnessed among the Catholic priests in Rome, Luther decided he wanted no part of this deliberate abuse of authority.

Upon his return to Wittenberg, Luther lay hold on the Word of God and continued his meticulous study of Scripture. He went on to receive two bachelor's degrees in biblical studies and a doctorate of theology, subsequently accepting a teaching position on the theological faculty at the University of Wittenberg. The demands of preparation for delivering lectures drove Martin Luther to study the Word of God in even greater depth.

In the book of Romans, the apostle Paul tells of the *"righteousness of God."* Luther had always understood that phrase to mean that God was a righteous judge who demanded human righteousness. Now, Luther was beginning to understand righteousness as a gift of God's grace. This discovery set Luther afire. He had discovered, or recovered, the doctrine of justification by faith.

A spark ignited.

His awakening to the understanding of justification opened the divide between the Roman Catholic Church and himself. It led him to a fresh understanding of the doctrines of salvation. Luther finally found the assurance that had evaded him, and his critique of the theological world around him was beginning to take shape.

For Martin Luther, salvation could not be found in the membership within an institution or in the hands of human beings. Rather, he saw it as a spiritual gift directly from God to the individual. Salvation was grounded in faith, and this faith was what led to salvation through the grace of God. God's grace was a sovereign gift that was available, irrespective of one's actions or good deeds. Grace was that enabling power given by God that would allow a person to receive salvation. According to Luther, that grace was not predicated on church membership or earthly works. It was a gift that had been established on the Cross by the death of Jesus Christ, only attainable through one's faith in Christ and that finished work.

Luther concluded that the Roman Catholic Church had lost its fundamental understanding of salvation. In fact, the church had lost sight of several central, spiritual truths. He realized that a major reason for his lifelong spiritual torment was false teaching from the church. How can any man know when he's done enough to please God? It was all beginning to make sense. With joy in this new revelation, Martin Luther began teaching that salvation is a gift of God's grace, received by faith in God's promise to forgive us because of Christ's death on the Cross.

In 1517, Pope Leo X announced a new round of indulgences to financially cover the construction of St. Peter's Basilica in Rome. The selling of indulgences even became a full-time profession for some within the Catholic Church, and although discouraged throughout Germany, the practice continued unabated.

A Dominican priest named Johann Tetzel was appointed to sell these indulgences in Germany. Tetzel was zealous about his job, and he commissioned wholesale retailing of these indulgences. And while these new indulgences for the construction of St. Peter's Basilica were not sold in Luther's province, his parishioners began to flock to Tetzel. Luther became outraged when his own congregation began to present indulgences they had purchased as documentation of their forgiven sins. Forgiveness could not be bought. It was a free gift of God's mercy. He resented the exploitation of his people and saw this as an outright offense to salvation.

But, the controversy was much more involved than just the sale of indulgences. Fury mounted in Luther's heart over the brazen attempts of the church to sell salvation. Committed to the idea that salvation could be reached through faith alone, Luther translated his convictions to the tip of his pen. Hoping for discussion and ultimately change, Luther came up with 95 points of contention that would need to be resolved for the church to be purged of this great fallacy. These 95 points became more commonly known as Martin Luther's Ninety-Five Theses.

Luther's Ninety-Five Theses started a religious revolution. From the time Luther first began to question church authority to the moment he laid pen to paper, all he really wanted was answers. His goal was to expose the errors that had taken hold of the church, plead for reform, and spark a debate. Revolution was not entirely on his mind. He merely yearned for a spiritual revival, but you can't have revival before you have a reformation.

One could think of the Ninety-Five Theses as a map to the truth that Luther himself had re-discovered. He wasn't bringing about something new or unchartered; he was merely uncovering the truth that had been hidden for so long.

Romans 1:17 says, *"For therein is the righteousness of God revealed from faith to faith: as it is written, The just shall live by faith."* And then, Ephesians 2:8 states, *"For by grace are ye saved through faith; and that not of yourselves: it is the gift of God."*

Martin Luther used these verses of Scripture as his compass to the truth. He was hoping to light the way for the church to follow and return to that truth—the truth that justification is by grace through faith alone and not by works. He wrote with fervor, but he also wrote with hope—the hope of change.

On October 31, 1517, Martin Luther boldly nailed his Ninety-Five Theses to the door of Castle Church in Wittenberg, Germany, unveiling a collection of 95 scathing attacks against the Roman Catholic Church and the authority of the pope.

Although the document contained a humble and academic tone, Luther's accusations were rigid, and it laid out a devastating critique of the Catholic Church. At the forefront was the sale of indulgences, which turned salvation into a commercial transaction rather than a genuine repentance of sin.

The Ninety-Five Theses posed questions that many wanted to ask, but few had dared to proclaim publicly. It also became a tangible foothold for those growing discontented with the Catholic Church. Did the church hold the keys to heaven as they claimed? Was the pope infallible? Did indulgences remove all sin? Was excommunication the same as eternal damnation? Luther had called the church into account, and for many, they would be hard-pressed to answer in a convincing manner.

Martin Luther held two advantages that previous reformers had lacked: The recent invention of Guttenberg's printing press and a rise in literacy throughout the Holy Roman Empire. Luther published thousands of pamphlets that set forth his position against the Catholic Church. These pamphlets quickly spread throughout Europe, inevitably making their way to Rome.

When this document came into the hands of Pope Leo X, its reception was cold. He ordered the vicar-general of the Augustinian Order to silence its monks, but Luther would not go quietly.

After several months of continued protest against the church, Pope Leo X grew tired of Luther's antics, knowing he must put an end to this act of defiance.

In 1518, Luther was summoned by Pope Leo X to appear in Heidelberg, Germany, to defend his statements. Martin Luther debated a panel of distinguished Augustinian monks, who were considered to be theological masters of the church.

The monks were no match for Luther.

Months later, Cardinal Cajetan put Martin Luther on trial. Cajetan, also a distinguished scholar, was no more a match against Luther than the Augustinian monks. While the cardinal defended the Catholic Church's use of indulgences, Luther set out his countering positions with great precision and was unfazed by feeble attempts at belittling his courage. Luther said he would not recant anything unless Scripture proved him wrong. "I deny that the pope is above Scripture. His Holiness abuses Scripture."

Cardinal Cajetan lost his temper and began shouting at Luther, demanding Luther to leave and to never darken his holy door again unless he was willing to say, "I recant."

In due time, a series of commissions was convened to examine Luther's teachings. The first papal commission found them to be heretical, but the second merely stated that Luther's writings were scandalous and offensive to pious ears. But, Pope Leo X had all he could take of Martin Luther. In 1520, he issued a "papal bull"—a public declaration that concluded Luther's propositions as heresy. The papal bull not only obliged all Christians to acknowledge the pope's authority and power to grant indulgences, but also threatened Luther with excommunication from the Catholic Church and gave him 120 days to recant in Rome. No sooner than Luther received the bull, he burned it—publicly!

When Pope Leo X received word of Luther's active defiance, he issued a "Decet Romanum Pontificem," in English meaning,

"It Pleases the Roman Pontiff," thus banishing Luther from the church. The issue was turned over to secular authorities, and Luther agreed to appear before the Diet of Worms.

As vast as the rift now appeared between Martin Luther and the church, there was still a chance for reprieve, and Luther was prepared to address the accusations against him. This was to be Luther's defining moment.

After a long and difficult journey from Wittenberg, Luther arrived in Worms with great fanfare. Preceding his arrival, a crowd of 2,000 lined the streets to escort him into town. The citizens eagerly pressed forth to see this man, every moment the crowds increasing. The procession made its way with difficulty through the multitudes. A great number even climbed onto rooftops to catch a glimpse. The tops of houses and the pavements of the streets were littered with spectators. To some, he was a prodigy of wisdom; to others, a fool. Nonetheless, the entire city came to see him.

Luther advanced through the crowds with difficulty as he made his way into the town hall. Luther's appearance before the Diet in itself was a great victory over the church and the papacy. The pope had condemned him to perpetual silence, yet, here he was, about to speak before thousands of attentive listeners.

Approaching the assembly, Luther was presented with a table littered with copies of his own writings. The panel of dignitaries demanded confirmation that he authored the various writings attributed to him and whether he espoused of its contents. Luther calmly stated, "The books are all mine, and I have written more."

The Diet further noted that Luther's writings contained the errors of previous reformers and that various councils had already condemned these heretics over past centuries. Luther was undeterred. He demanded that these men show him any Scripture that would refute his positions and writings. There was none.

"You have not answered the question put to you," one of the dignitaries said. "You were not summoned hither to call in question the decisions of councils. You are required to give a clear and precise answer. Will you, or will you not retract?"

Luther responded, "Since then your serene majesty and your lordships request a simple reply, I will give it without horns and hoofs, and say: Unless I am convinced by the testimony of Scripture or by plain reason (for I believe in neither the pope nor in councils alone, for it is well-known, not only that they have erred, but also have contradicted themselves), I am mastered by the passages of Scripture which I have quoted, and my conscience is captive to the Word of God. I cannot and will not recant, for it is neither safe nor honest to violate one's conscience. I can do no other. Here I take my stand, God being my helper. Amen."

The assembly, including the Holy Roman Emperor, Charles V, was thunderstruck. They witnessed firsthand Luther's bold demeanor and unshaken courage. The monk, who so courageously nailed his Ninety-Five Theses to the door of the Castle Church nearly four years prior, had braved his enemies amongst an assembly of men who thirsted for his blood. Dumbfounded but still seeking grounds to convict Luther, the Diet convened to deliberate. After several days of deliberation, the assembly was faced with coming to a decision on Luther's fate.

Without validation, Charles V issued the "Edict of Worms," placing Luther under imperial ban, banning his literature and officially declaring him a heretic to the entirety of the Holy Roman Empire. He was to be arrested on site. Furthermore, the assembly sanctioned his death with no legal consequences under the law. Essentially, the Roman Catholic Church was condoning the murder of Martin Luther.

The Edict of Worms further stated that it would be considered a crime for anyone within the empire to give Luther sanctuary.

But, Luther had already vanished.

His sentence came down several days after the Diet, so Luther, now a condemned and wanted man, had already taken shelter, thanks to Prince Frederick of Saxony, who whisked him into hiding at Wartburg Castle days before the edict was made public.

In exile, Martin Luther confined himself to Wartburg Castle—a massive and hauntingly beautiful structure, built in 1068. The castle, located atop a steep hill overlooking the city of Eisenach, Germany, kept Martin Luther out of the limelight for more than a year.

While there, Luther grew out his hair and his beard, and he took on a new identity as 'Knight George.' He was able to avoid capture, continuing his doctrinal attacks against the Catholic Church, all the while creating a new branch of Christianity—what we call "Protestant theology." But, while in hiding, the devil continued to fight him hard. Since childhood, he had been pestered by demon spirits, but it grew worse over time and only intensified during his stay at Wartburg Castle.

Luther held fast to prayer and worship to ward off these evil attacks, but Luther wrote of one account where he was awakened in the middle of the night by a vicious attack from the devil. During the assault, Luther defended himself by throwing an inkwell at him. To this day, it is said that there is still an ink stain on the wall in the room where Luther stayed.

Martin Luther also began work on translating the New Testament into German, which he derived from a collection of original Hebrew and Greek manuscripts, known as "Textus Receptus." Although many failed to see the true spiritual condition of the Catholic Church, Luther provided an answer to their dilemma, which was their lack of access to the Word of God. It was this translation by Luther that spurred the monumental expansion of the Word of God to the common man. By 1534, Luther yielded a complete German translation. This contribution was not only revolutionary in his day but also in theological history. It sparked a chain of events that ultimately led to the King James Bible—a translation still in use today.

Martin Luther was the right man, with the right message, at the right time. It was his valiant efforts that led to the spreading of the Protestant Reformation throughout the European landscape and beyond.

Luther's courageous fight also paved the way for countless others to follow his footsteps in taking a stand against the Holy Roman Empire and its corrupt hierarchy. One of those men was a brilliant theologian named William Tyndale. He enrolled at Oxford in 1506 and received his master's degree by the age of 21. He proved to be a gifted linguist, learning a bevy of languages during his time at the university, including Hebrew, German, Latin, Spanish, French, Italian, Greek, and English. One of his associates remarked that Tyndale was so equally skilled in each language, it might be difficult to tell which one was his native tongue.

By 1520, Tyndale had completely attached himself to the doctrines of the Reformation, devoting his life to the study of the Scriptures, more so after he heard a Roman Catholic clergyman remark, "We are better to be without God's laws than the pope's."

Tyndale traveled to Germany in 1524, where he crossed paths with Martin Luther and likely received his assistance in translating his own English version of the Bible. His literary activity during this time was unprecedented. Taking advantage of the recent invention of Guttenberg's printing press, Tyndale churned out a number of original compositions including, "A Pathway into the Holy Scripture," "The Parable of the Wicked Mammon," and "The Obedience of a Christian Man."

Tyndale's noble efforts, however, came with great contention from the Roman Catholic Church, and, eventually, his naysayers caught up with him. We do not know who planned and financed the plot that captured him, but we do know that it was carried out by Henry Phillips, a man who had been accused of robbing his own father and gambling himself into poverty. Phillips befriended Tyndale, becoming a regular guest at meals, and was one of the few privileged to hold Tyndale's compositions in his hands, proving to be a fatal error in Tyndale's judgment of trust. One night, Phillips lured Tyndale away from the safety of his quarters and directly into the arms of soldiers. He was arrested and immediately ushered to the Castle of Vilvoorde, where he was imprisoned for more than 500 days.

Trials for heresy were in the hands of special commissioners of the Holy Roman Empire, and it took several months for the law to take its course. After 16 months of imprisonment, one might assume that Tyndale had many an hour to reflect on the Scriptures and his own writings. You might imagine that this passage in particular from one of his tracts gave him a great source of comfort: "Let it not make thee despair, neither yet discourage thee, O reader, that it is forbidden thee in pain of life and goods, or that it is made breaking of the king's peace, or treason unto his highness, to read the Word of thy soul's health—for if God be on our side, what matter maketh it who be against us, be they bishops, cardinals, popes."

Tyndale was eventually charged with heresy. He was condemned to death and executed on October 6, 1536. As his lifeless body was being burned at the stake, he uttered his final words, "Lord, open the king of England's eyes." Three years later, his prayer would be answered with the publication of King Henry VIII's "Great Bible."

Tyndale's influence continued to flourish. In 1611, drawing from Tyndale's translation, 54 scholars produced the King James Version of the Bible. Nearly 90 percent of the King James Version can be attributed to Tyndale's Bible. Additionally, new words and phrases were introduced in the King James. "Let there be light," "the powers that be," "filthy lucre," and "it came to pass" were all derived from Tyndale's translation.

Another man who dared to take a stand against the Roman Catholic Church was John Calvin. Calvin was a French scholar who became the impetus for the Protestant Reformation in Geneva, Switzerland.

> I saw that many were hungering and thirsting after Christ and yet that only a few had any real knowledge of Him. —John Calvin

But, before his spiritual transformation took place, Calvin acquiesced to his father's wishes to pursue a career in law. He studied more than five years at the University of Orleans, attaining distinction in a subject he felt little or no passion for. He also studied Renaissance humanism, learned Greek, and excelled in philosophy.

Then, word of Martin Luther's teaching reached France. His life made an abrupt turn.

> God tamed to teachableness a mind too stubborn for its years—for I was strongly devoted to the superstitions of the papacy that nothing less could draw me from such depths of mire. And so this mere taste of true godliness that I received set me on fire with such a desire to progress that I pursued the rest of my studies more coolly. —John Calvin

Believing in the sovereignty and providence of God, Calvin now viewed the Roman Catholic Church and its corrupt bureaucracy as a mockery of God's grace. With intense persecution on his heels, Calvin was forced to flee France and seek refuge across the border in Geneva. He didn't intend to stay in Geneva for long, but the Lord had a different plan.

> I felt as if God from heaven had laid His mighty hand upon me to stop me in my course—and I was so terror stricken that I did not continue my journey. —John Calvin

Leading a new movement of reformation, Calvin directed the attack against the Catholic Church, opposing its beliefs, rituals, hierarchy, and the unjust power of the papal office.

It was at this time that he penned one of the most influential documents in Western history: *Institutes of the Christian Religion*. In the book, Calvin focuses on the sovereignty of God and outlines his views on the church and Christian liberty.

Calvin portrayed the true spirit of reformation. He often drove himself beyond his body's limits to preach the Word. When he could no longer walk, he was carried in a chair to the pulpit. When his doctor forbade him to go out in the winter air to preach, he crowded people into his own bedroom and preached there. To those who would urge him to rest, he asked, "What? Would you have the Lord find me idle when He comes?"

John Calvin passed away in 1564 at the age of 54.

John Calvin's protégé, a Scotsman named John Knox, also rose to prominence as a reformer in the mid-16TH century. Knox studied theology at the University of St. Andrews and was ordained in 1536. After gaining a healthy reputation for preaching, he too, faced intense persecution and was forced to flee to France once Mary Tudor took the throne. He eventually made his way to Geneva, where he met John Calvin. Knox was so impressed with the city, he called it, "The most perfect school of Christ that was ever on earth since the days of the apostles."

Knox didn't stay in Geneva for long; his heart was for Scotland. But, the spiritual influence he felt from John Calvin and the people of Geneva made a definitive impact in his life. Knox eventually returned to his homeland to complete his lifework: preaching the good news of Jesus Christ and Him crucified.

A warrior for his cause, Knox was known to carry a sword with him at times. Willing to sacrifice his life for his faith, he would become a leader of the Scottish Revolution against the Catholic Church. Knox was instrumental in the abolishment of the pope's jurisdiction in the Scottish Parliament. The establishment of the Church of Scotland led to reformed theology and the foundation of a new denomination—Presbyterianism.

Surrounded by family and friends in the comfort of his home, John Knox passed away in 1572 at the age of 58. Just before his eyes closed, he asked his wife to read from the Bible. She turned to Paul's first epistle to the Corinthians: *"That no flesh should glory in his presence. But of Him are ye in Christ Jesus, who of God is made unto us wisdom, and righteousness, and sanctification, and redemption"* (I Cor. 1:29-30).

The Reformation stands today as a testament to God's grace. It is also a constant reminder that no earthly authority can overthrow the divine power of God's Word. Romans 13:1 says, *"Let every soul be subject unto the higher powers. For there is no power but of God: the powers that be are ordained of God."*

History reminds us that this movement came with a heavy cost. Thousands gave their own lives for this cause, but because these reformers were bold enough to act upon their convictions, the unrelenting struggle they faced allowed for the progression of freedom and liberty for anyone who chooses to accept it. That freedom is the Word of God—the very freedom that still resounds in our world today.

Many reformers carried the torch during the course of the Reformation, but no one attained such prominence as Martin Luther. Luther was a fundamental force of nature, embodied in spiritual truth, offering a simple, yet paramount, vision for salvation, which resonated with so many people. His central teachings—that the Word of God is the only source of spiritual authority and that salvation is reached through faith alone—shaped the very core of Protestantism. And it was his translation of the Bible into the language of his people that radically changed the relationship between preachers and their parishioners.

Just before his death in 1546, he said, "When I die, I want to be a ghost ... So I can continue to pester the bishops, priests, and godless monks until they have more trouble with a dead Luther than they could have had before with a thousand living ones."

The nailing of his Ninety-Five Theses was a remarkable milestone that will live on in church history for ages to come, should the Lord tarry. This document single-handedly fractured the very fabric of the Roman Catholic Church and forever changed the course of Christianity. The Protestant church's calendar is filled with "holy days," but none are more central to its existence than that of October 31—Reformation Day. On this day, the world celebrates what they call "All Hallows Eve," but we who are saved celebrate Martin Luther's Ninety-Five Theses.

Even today, Luther remains a significant presence in theological discussions all around the world, not just for his devotion to biblical principles, but, also, for his *insistence* on the matter. The courage and willingness of this man to risk death for his beliefs makes Luther, without a doubt, one of the greatest emancipators in human history.

Martin Luther wasn't perfect. None of us are. Luther would even grow to regret some of the ill consequences of the movement he inspired. The sweeping changes that occurred were highly resisted, and religious wars broke out in high numbers as kings and princes began moving away from the authority of the Catholic Church. The Thirty Years' War, for example, was one of the most destructive conflicts in European history as Catholics and Protestants battled for power and territory. Nearly 40 percent of Germany's population was slaughtered, and more than 100 years passed before there was any hint of reconciliation between these two institutions.

Furthermore, Martin Luther's rhetoric was often anti-Semitic. He denounced the Jewish people and urged for their harsh persecution.

"Be on your guard against the Jews," Luther exclaimed, "Knowing that wherever they have their synagogues, nothing is found but a den of devils, in which sheer self-glory, conceit, lies, blasphemy, and defaming of God are practiced."

Still, if not for Luther's convictions, the Reformation never would have changed the spiritual and political landscape of the world. His actions transitioned Christianity from a religion with one omnipotent power—the Catholic Church—to a spiritual movement encompassing a myriad of new beliefs, evolving into Protestant denominations. Though some are based on differing scriptural interpretations, there is a common thread that unifies them all: the gospel of Jesus Christ, faith in His finished work, and the freedom it bears.

William Bradford prays upon the Pilgrims' arrival at Plymouth.

CHAPTER 2

THEY DESIRE A BETTER COUNTRY

CHAPTER TWO

THEY DESIRE A BETTER COUNTRY

"To every thing there is a season, and a time to every purpose under the heaven: A time to be born, and a time to die; a time to plant, and a time to pluck up that which is planted; A time to kill, and a time to heal; a time to break down, and a time to build up; A time to weep, and a time to laugh; a time to mourn, and a time to dance; A time to cast away stones, and a time to gather stones together; a time to embrace, and a time to refrain from embracing; A time to get, and a time to lose; a time to keep, and a time to cast away; A time to rend, and a time to sew; a time to keep silence, and a time to speak; A time to love, and a time to hate; a time of war, and a time of peace." (Eccl. 3:1-8).

At some point in our lives, we all must learn the lesson that God's timing is just as important as God's will.

In 1492, an Italian named Christopher Columbus set off into the western horizon in hopes of discovering a new trade route to the West Indies. After months at sea, Columbus dropped anchor, only he wasn't in the West Indies, he was in a whole new world—the Americas. Though many historians contend over the true intentions of his voyage, Columbus did write *this* prior to leaving Spain:

> It was the Lord who put it into my mind. I could feel His hand upon me – There is no question that the inspiration was from the Holy Spirit, because He comforted me with rays of marvelous illumination from the Holy Scriptures – No one should fear to undertake a task in the name of our Savior, if it is just and if the intention is purely for His service. The fact that the Gospel must still be preached to so many lands in such a short time; this is what convinces me. — Christopher Columbus

When Columbus set foot on solid ground after traversing the great Atlantic, it may have been a small step for him, but it was a giant leap for mankind. Most of the world believed as fact that the world was flat. Now, Columbus had proof that the world was anything but.

Like Sir Isaac Newton and his realization of gravity with a falling apple, or Benjamin Franklin's discovery of electricity by simply flying a kite in a thunderstorm, from one moment to the next, the world was changing. When Columbus returned to Europe, he sent shock waves throughout the civilized world with news of this new and exotic land.

European colonization of the New World followed several key developments during the 16TH century. Nautical discoveries made ships safer and faster while crossing the Atlantic; new technologies like the first camera were invented; and medical advances like the first toilet improved health and hygiene.

Why are we talking about the inventions of the 16TH century? Good question. Often in looking back and studying history, we also hope to learn something about ourselves. Sometimes we forget that we have the luxury of hindsight, and most times, the conditions in which people lived were far different from those that we are accustomed. Let's be honest: To think of life without air-conditioning, supermarkets, cell phones, satellites, and the Internet would make most of us a little uncomfortable. We must keep that in mind when we speak of the colonists. They didn't have a hardware store if a tool was broken and no hospital to bring the injured. Think about it. Think about the faith of these men and women: to completely uproot their lives and families, to journey a perilous crossing, only to find themselves in an unknown land.

THE STORY OF JAMESTOWN

"The wicked shall be turned into hell, and all the nations that forget God" (Ps. 9:17).

London, England, December 1606: Three small ships—*Susan Constant, Discovery, and Godspeed*—carrying 105 men in total, set sail for the New World.

On this voyage was a stocky, red-haired soldier of fortune named John Smith. He possessed all the qualities of a powerful leader—bold, charming, quick-witted—and had built quite the reputation as a world traveler. At the age of 16, a young John Smith decided to join the military. For more than a decade, he displayed prowess in battle and a unique ability to lead men. Smith quickly climbed through the ranks and became a mercenary captain.

But, he was no more than an ordinary passenger on this expedition to the New World, and his arrogance pervaded the ship. His abrasiveness became so bothersome on the voyage that his fellow passengers placed him in shackles. Smith was charged with mutiny, and the ship's captain, Christopher Newport, planned to execute him when they reached the shores of America.

Fortunately for Smith, an unsealed box containing orders from the Virginia Company, a joint stock enterprise chartered by King James I, appointed him as one of the leaders, thus sparing him from the gallows. The passengers were dismayed to find Smith's name on the list, but through his charm, they wound up electing him council president of their new colony. John Smith may have arrived to the New World in cuffs, but he stepped off the ship in command.

The English were already involved in planting settlements in Ireland, but they acknowledged the limitations of these Irish colonies, and they were lusting for new land and new opportunity. Interest in America was growing, and the Virginia Company was in search of immediate profits. They were expecting gains from gold, iron, timber, and many of the other abundant natural resources.

After four storm-tossed months at sea, Captain John Smith's fleet of weathered vessels finally reached the Virginia shore near

Chesapeake Bay. On May 6, 1607, the settlers named their new colony Jamestown in honor of their English ruler, King James I.

They were astonished at the beauty of the place. It was springtime in Virginia. Warm weather, soft breezes, dogwood trees in full blossom, greenery enveloping the landscape — they might have thought they landed in the garden of Eden.

In the days that followed, the men built a fort, a storehouse, a collection of thatched huts, and a church. It was the perfect time of year to start planting crops; however, none of the colonists knew how. In preparation for their expedition, the Virginia Company had gathered a group of skilled and educated artisans to build a new colony but overlooked the need for woodsmen and farmers. Having no knowledge of agriculture, they had no way of exploiting the area's abundance in game and fish.

The natives, on the other hand, did have the knowledge and skills that the colonists lacked. In fact, the tribes surrounding Jamestown were largely an agricultural people focused on raising corn. But instead of asking for help, John Smith and his band of lethargic men resorted to attacking their villages to curtail their food shortage. The Indians turned hostile against these crude English intruders and countered with their own raids to protect their land and save their people.

Chief Powhatan was the powerful, charismatic leader of the numerous Algonquian-speaking tribes that surrounded Jamestown, representing over 10,000 natives. They lived along rivers in fortified settlements and resided in wood houses, sheathed with bark. Chief Powhatan wanted to develop trade with Jamestown, exchanging corn and hides for hatchets, swords, and muskets, but the colonists intended to seize his lands and enslave his people.

As summer approached, the heat and humidity grew steadily more oppressive, and, thus, the true face of Jamestown began to emerge.

The only drinking water came from the river. At low tide it was foul; at high tide it was salty from ocean water creeping upriver. Looking for fresh water, they dug wells too close to their waste disposal area. Disease, namely typhoid fever, became rampant.

Mosquitos began to surface. Rising in swarms from the swamps, they brought the scourge of malaria, which took its toll on the defenseless colonists. Men began dying at a horrific rate, sometimes three or four in a single night.

One night, a towering fire tore through the already battered settlement. Within minutes, most of their provisions—tents, blankets, bedding, clothes—and all but three of their huts were consumed. With winter approaching, more lives were likely to be lost before shelter could be resurrected.

While most of the colonists were cursing at God for their misfortunes, John Smith took note of the example set by Robert Hunt, Jamestown's only preacher.

> None did ever hear him repine of his loss. Hunt seemed willing to suffer the loss of all things in order to gain Christ.
> —John Smith

> Almighty God, we beseech Thee to bless us and this plantation which we have begun in Thy fear and for Thy glory ...

> And seeing, Lord, the highest end of our plantation here is to set up the standard and display the banner of Jesus Christ, even here where Satan's throne is, Lord, let our labor be blessed in laboring for the conversion of the heathen. ... Lord, sanctify our spirits and give us holy hearts, that so we may be Thy instruments in this most glorious work. —Robert Hunt

For the colonists at Jamestown, Robert Hunt's sermons were merely a form of entertainment and a means for passing the time. They often mocked his work ethic and ridiculed his spiritual courage. Helplessly lazy and not wanting to work in the fields, the other men scoffed at the notion of manual labor. They put all of their hopes in supply ships from England—supply ships that would not soon come.

By the spring of 1609, a rat infestation began ravaging the struggling settlement, destroying most of what crops they did have. Staring at the soggy, putrid mess before them, they realized the scope of the disaster: they had no food at all.

The settlers had been hungry before, but never had it been this bad. All of their livestock had been consumed—hogs, sheep, goats, chickens, horses. Next went the dogs and cats, field mice, snakes, and the rats that had destroyed their corn.

The colonists resorted to digging up the roots of trees and shrubs. They ate every bit of shoe leather they could get their hands on. Some fled to nearby Indian villages, seeking refuge, only to be burned at the stake. Others dug up fresh corpses, cut them into stew meat, and boiled them. One man murdered another and feasted on his remains. Still, it was not enough.

These men had put all of their faith in fame and fortune, expecting to find gold, friendly natives, and easy living. Instead, they found disease, dissension, and death. Of the original 105 men, only 38 remained. Yet, even after all their hardships, the remaining survivors continued to turn away from the face of God. Jamestown was sowing the seeds of its own destruction.

Death again took its toll, but this time, it was Robert Hunt. The colony was now stripped of its sole source of spiritual comfort. Like a smoldering fire taking its final breaths and extinguishing into a bed of embers, Jamestown was left in complete darkness.

Famished and desperate for survival, Captain John Smith led a small group of men up the James River on a corn-stealing expedition, once again trespassing onto Chief Powhatan's territory. But, Smith and his men, ill-prepared, were ambushed. Most of the men were executed on the spot. Smith was merely wounded but had been captured and brought to the chief for interrogation.

Chief Powhatan instructed the Indians to bind Smith with rope and prepare him for execution. For once, Smith's charm and quick wit had failed him. He was powerless until out of nowhere, Chief Powhatan's 11-year-old daughter, Pocahontas, intervened, making a dramatic appeal for his life.

Pocahontas was a favorite of her father's. He often referred to her publicly as his "delight and darling," so it is of little doubt that she held a great power of persuasion with him. In fact, the chief was so moved by her gesture of goodwill, he agreed to release John Smith in exchange for muskets, hatchets, and other trinkets.

Schoolchildren still learn of the dramatic tale of Pocahontas intervening to save John Smith's life. Such climactic events are endearing. They animate history, inspire movies, and excite our imagination, yet they are often exaggerated. Pocahontas and John Smith were never in love. God merely used Pocahontas to give John Smith and Jamestown one final chance at redemption.

For the weeks following, Pocahontas often visited the Jamestown settlement once or twice a week to supply provisions for Smith and the remaining colonists. Despite the connection, there is very little in historical records to suggest a romantic link between John Smith and Pocahontas.

Slowly, the colony began to repair, but Jamestown took yet another hit when John Smith injured himself with an accidental gunpowder explosion. Selfishly, he chose to retreat back to England, abandoning Jamestown and leaving the leaderless colony in a state of total disorder.

John Smith remained in England for the remainder of his life and focused on a career in writing. He published a number of books that detailed his time abroad—*The General History of Virginia, The True Travels, Adventures, and Observations of Captain John Smith,* and *A Description of New England*—pushing for the colonization of America.

In *A Description of New England,* Smith illustrates America as an ideal environment for monetary opportunity in the form of industry, including fishing, farming, shipbuilding, and fur trading. But, he didn't sugarcoat depictions of America in order to heighten its appeal. He wished for potential colonists to be aware of the dangers they faced, the hard work that colonization would require, and the benefits they stood to gain. Rather than making false promises of abounding gold to appease his readers, Smith attempted to attract interest for colonization by depicting the opportunities that fertile soil and abundant resources would bring. He stressed that only those with a strong work ethic would be able to reap the benefits of America in the face of danger.

The new colonial regime that took over Jamestown after John Smith's departure resumed attacks on the surrounding Native American tribes. On one occasion, these men even went so far as to capture an Indian woman and her children, marching them to a nearby river, shooting them in the head one by one, and tossing them into the water, left to drown. Eventually, Pocahontas was kidnapped herself, but as the weeks passed, she surprised her captors by choosing to join them. She embraced Christianity, was renamed "Rebecca," and fell in love with English colonist, John Rolfe.

The colony limped along for numerous years until it finally found a lucrative source of revenue—tobacco. As tobacco production boomed, so did the population. Men and women alike joined the veteran colonists and brought their own set of professional skills to help grow the struggling colony.

It would have taken a much deeper reliance on God to successfully bring Jamestown through the ordeals they faced in the early years. God was there, and He did answer the prayers of those who sincerely wished to change their ways, but, sadly, those were few and far between. With the arrival of new colonists came more families and with them, their Christian values. God allowed Jamestown to flourish ... eventually. It just took a lot longer than it should have.

THE STORY OF PLYMOUTH

> A better country was never seen nor heard of, for here are a multitude of God's blessings. —Emmanuel Altham (Plymouth colonist)

William Bradford was born to William and Alice Bradford in the Yorkshire farming community of Austerfield, England, in 1590. Tragedy struck at a young age for young William. By the time he was 6 years old, death had claimed both his mother and his father. For years, he was shuttled from house-to-house and town-to-town among several relatives.

As an orphan, William quickly learned to rely on the Word of God. The Bible was a great source of comfort to him, and he read it continuously, eventually giving his heart to Christ upon learning of God's forgiveness and the gift of eternal life. Even as a child, young William was able to discern the unbiblical nature of the Church of England.

The Puritan church that Bradford attended belonged to the most radical sect of Puritans – the Separatists. According to the Separatists, the Church of England had retained far too many aspects of Catholicism following the Reformation. The Separatists intended to purify themselves of all Catholic influence.

Young William found the Separatists' fellowship and lack of rituals and traditions refreshing. These people spoke enthusiastically of experiencing a personal relationship with Jesus Christ, and they were on a divine mission to create a new church committed to the proper worship of God. Such rebellion against the ideals of the Church of England enraged King James I, and when he took the throne in 1603, he resolved to eliminate these nonconformists, all the while claiming divine rule.

> The Reformers labored to have the right worship of God & discipline of Christ established in the church, according to the simplicity of the gospel, without the mixture of man's inventions ... The Church of England, though under many colors & pretenses, endeavored to have the episcopal dignity with their large power & jurisdiction still retained; with all those courts, cannons, & ceremonies, together with all such livings, revenues, & subordinate officers, enabled them with lordly & tyrannous power to persecute the poor servants of God. —William Bradford

The older William became, the more persecution he began to witness from the Church of England and from home. Bradford's spiritual defection angered his relatives, but he knew what he was doing was right. In a letter to them, a 12-year-old Bradford wrote:

> Were I like to endanger my life, or consume my estate by any ungodly courses, your counsels to me were very seasonable, but you know that I have been diligent and provident in my

> calling, and not only desirous to augment what I have ... To part from which will be as great a cross as can befall me. Nevertheless, to keep a good conscience, and walk in such a way as God has prescribed in His Word, is a thing which I must prefer before you all, and above life itself. —William Bradford

Separatist church services were held in secret, and when the congregation learned that the king was gunning for them, they knew they had to leave England if they wanted to retain their freedoms. They fled east to Holland.

For 12 years, Bradford and the other exiles lived and worshipped freely in Holland until King James I found out where they were hiding. The king pressured the Dutch government to begin harassing the Separatists – first vocally, and then physically, as rocks were often heaved at them in the streets.

Fearing an uprising by the Dutch, the Separatists knew it was time to make another clean break, but this time, they would have to travel much further to seek freedom from affliction.

These brave men and women wished to create a biblically centered settlement for their people, and they wouldn't take no for an answer. And now they were about to engage in one of the greatest expeditions in human history – the arduous pilgrimage to the wild lands of America.

God had chosen the Pilgrims to become His temple in the New World. If they could not purify the church from within, they would set up a church of their own in America, hoping to be stepping-stones for those wishing to leave Europe in search of religious and civil freedom. William Bradford had faith that such a holy settlement would be a beacon of righteousness for all who sought true liberty.

Plymouth, England, September 1620: 102 men, women, and children cram aboard a tiny ship, the *Mayflower*.

From the very beginning, obstacles began to mount against them. The *Mayflower* struggled westward through fierce storms. The crowded ship rocked in the angry sea. All of the hatches had to be battened down. The lack of light and fresh air made it unbearable onboard. There was the constant crying of small children, and nearly all of the passengers became wretchedly seasick at some point. Add to it a diet of stale peas and wormy biscuits; the crossing became insufferable.

The sea-weary Pilgrims were forced to endure yet another ordeal—harassment from the ship's crew. The sailors had taken to mocking them unmercifully, and their crew leader had taken such a dislike to the Pilgrims that he would revel at their seasickness and delight in telling them how much he looked forward to sewing them in shrouds and heaving them into the sea. Ironically, he was one of only two who perished on the transatlantic voyage.

> And I may not omit here a special work of God's providence. There was a proud and very profane young man, one of the seamen, of a lusty, able body, which made him the more haughty; he would always be contemning the poor people in their sickness, and cursing them daily with grievous execrations, and did not let to tell them, that he

> hoped to help cast half of them overboard before they came to their journey's end, and to make merry with what they had; and if he were by any gently reproved, he would curse and swear most bitterly ... But it pleased God before they came half seas over, to smite this young man with a grievous disease, of which he died in a desperate manner, and so was himself the first that was thrown overboard. Thus his curses light on his own head; and it was an astonishment to all his fellows, for they noted it to be the just hand of God upon him. —William Bradford

By November, their voyage led them to Cape Cod, drastically thrown off course by the storms. After several days of trying to steer themselves south to their destination of Virginia, strong winter seas forced them to surrender to nature's fury and drop anchor at Provincetown Harbor.

> After some hours sailing, it began to snow & rain, & about the middle of the afternoon, the wind increased, & the sea became very rough, and we broke our rudder, & it was as much as two men could do to steer her with a couple of oars ... We broke our mast in three pieces, & our sail fell overboard, in a very grown sea, so as we had like to have been cast away; yet by God's mercy we recovered ourselves. —William Bradford

Since they couldn't make it to Virginia, the Pilgrims realized they would be settling outside the jurisdiction of any organized government, so before they even set foot off the

Mayflower, the Pilgrims entered into a formal agreement. This agreement, known as the "Mayflower Compact," was signed on November 11, 1620:

> In the name of God, Amen. We whose names are underwritten, the loyal subjects of our dread sovereign Lord, King James, by the grace of God, of Great Britain, France, and Ireland King, Defender of the Faith, etc.
>
> Having undertaken, for the glory of God, and advancement of the Christian faith, and honor of our King and Country, a voyage to plant the first colony in the northern parts of Virginia, do by these presents solemnly and mutually, in the presence of God, and one of another, covenant and combine our selves together into a civil body politic, for our better ordering and preservation and furtherance of the ends aforesaid; and by virtue hereof to enact, constitute, and frame such just and equal laws, ordinances, acts, constitutions and offices, from time to time, as shall be thought most meet and convenient for the general good of the Colony, unto which we promise all due submission and obedience.
>
> In witness whereof we have hereunder subscribed our names at Cape Cod, the eleventh of November, in the year of the reign of our sovereign lord, King James, of England, France, and Ireland, the eighteenth, and of Scotland the fifty-fourth, 1620.

The Mayflower Compact would become the cornerstone of American democracy. It marked the first time in history, since the children of Israel, in which free and equal men had come together to create their own new civil government based solely on the Word of God.

From the *Mayflower*, they stood there breathing the fresh air, gazing at the wild and untamed land before them, far different from the cultivated England they had left behind.

The wayworn Pilgrims, too exhausted to even think about the task at hand, thanked God that their three months at sea were over.

> Being thus arrived at good harbor and brought safe to land, we fell upon our knees & blessed the God of heaven, who had brought us over the vast & furious ocean, and delivered us from all the perils & miseries thereof ... But here I cannot but stay and make a pause, and stand half amassed at our poor present condition; being thus passed the vast ocean, and a sea of troubles before in our preparation, we had now no friends to welcome us, nor inns to entertain or refresh our weather-beaten bodies, no houses or much less towns to repair too to seek for help. —William Bradford

Pilgrim settlers formed exploration parties to venture the unknown lands of the coast. For weeks, these groups searched for an ideal location to establish a secure settlement.

On December 26, 1620, they discovered a suitable site to begin their colony.

> We marched into this land & found diverse cornfields, & little running brooks. So we returned to our ship again with this news to the rest of our people, which did much comfort their hearts. —William Bradford

The Pilgrims named the site after the English town from which they departed: Plimouth.

As the Pilgrims explored their newfound home, a number of promising discoveries came to light. Providentially, the location featured a prominent hill ideal for a defensive fort, four spring-fed creeks with the sweetest water any of them had ever tasted, and an open hillside that had already been cleared and readied to plant. The soil was rich and fertile, capable of supporting a wide variety of crops.

But, having arrived in the midst of winter, planting was futile. A shortage of food plagued the weary Pilgrims. Bitter cold gave way to frostbite. Malnutrition and disease, namely scurvy, began to take its toll. The Pilgrims begin dying—six in December, eight in January. They were falling like casualties on a battlefield, and in a sense, that was what they were—locked in a life-or-death struggle with Satan himself. But, the more adversity that mounted against them, the harder they prayed, never giving in to pain or despair. As their ranks thinned, they drew closer together, strengthening their faith all the more. After that first fateful winter, only half of the Pilgrims had survived.

> And of these in the time of most distress, there was but 6 or 7 sound persons, who, to their great commendations be it

> spoken, spared no pains, night nor day, but with abundance of toil and hazard of their own health, fetched us wood, made us fires, dressed us meat, made our beds, washed our loathsome clothes, clothed & unclothed us ... And all this willingly & cheerfully, without any grudging in the least, showing herein their true love unto their friends & brethren - a rare example & worthy to be remembered. —William Bradford

The Pilgrims were the founding fathers to *the* Founding Fathers. By their faith, they were setting the cornerstone for the church in America.

The struggles that the Pilgrims faced that winter were, without a doubt, grueling, but they knew that the will of God is not always a path of ease and comfort. Sometimes God will test our perseverance with trial and adversity in order to develop our faith and reliance in Him. Lucky for us, the Pilgrims had a wealth of it.

If anyone's faith was tested, it was that of William Bradford. When the Mayflower arrived in the New World and anchored off the coast, it took several weeks of expeditions to find a suitable place to start their colony. While Bradford was on one of these expeditions, his wife, Dorothy, fell off the ship into the freezing waters of Provincetown Harbor and drowned. Many men would've chosen to return to England after such a heavy loss, but he chose to stay. God had a plan for William Bradford.

Another man who withstood the adversity of that harsh winter was the captain of the *Mayflower,* Christopher Jones. Not a Pilgrim himself, Captain Jones never intended to stay in

Plymouth for long, but the biting cold and unrelenting snowfall forced him and his crew to endure that winter, as well, until conditions improved. Once the warmth of spring had calmed the seas, he was finally able to leave the colony behind. But, before he left, Captain Jones saw the struggles at hand for the Pilgrims, so he granted them an invitation to return with him to England. Even after all of their trials and tribulations, not one person accepted the captain's request—not one.

One can only imagine the anxiety and uncertainty that plagued these pioneers—weary, worn, hungry—and it wasn't just men and women. These people were literally giving their children's lives up to the will of God, but with faith as their foundation, they trusted in God's righteousness to provide.

As the *Mayflower* disappeared into the horizon, the Pilgrims who survived that fateful winter must have realized the gravity of this moment: The ship that brought them there was now leaving. There was no turning back.

While the colonists at Jamestown had resorted to stealing, killing, and savagery to satisfy their hunger, the faithful Pilgrims of Plymouth Colony would handle their situation in a starkly different manner.

Had the Pilgrims arrived in Plymouth some three years earlier, they would have been met by a fierce tribe of Native Americans known as the Patuxet. These Indians brutally murdered any outsiders who landed on their shores, but in 1617, it is believed that a mysterious plague completely devastated the tribe. William Bradford would later write that the bones of the dead were scattered throughout the colony upon their arrival.

With their first winter behind them and food becoming scarce, the Pilgrims knew they had to start planting crops in order to survive. Death had claimed the men who had any knowledge of farming, and the survivors didn't have any idea what to do, but they continued to lean on the Scriptures.

"And the children of Israel did eat manna forty years, until they came to a land inhabited; they did eat manna, until they came unto the borders of the land of Canaan" (Ex. 16:35).

Just as God sent manna from heaven to the Israelites, God was about to send the Pilgrims a miraculous gift of their own.

"Indian coming!" One of the men spotted a native in the distance just as the colonists were finishing an afternoon meeting in the common house.

Everyone rushed to the window to peer at this tall, well-built Indian, wearing nothing but a leather loincloth, striding down the main road, bold and confident. He was headed straight for the common house. The colonists were bewildered.

"What was this lone native doing, strolling through the middle of their camp in broad daylight," they might've thought.

Bradford opened the door slowly. The Indian was only steps away. Suddenly, he stopped and stood there motionless, expressionless, just staring at the colonists. They exchanged glances at each other as if they had both just seen a ghost. Only a gentle breeze could break the silence.

Finally, the Indian spoke up, "Welcome Englishmen! I am Samoset. Do you have any beer?"

The Pilgrims were speechless. They were expecting trouble from the natives. Instead, they found a friendly Indian that not only spoke perfect English but, also, came in peace. Samoset's request was denied, but a helping of biscuits, pudding, and roast duck were generously offered, which Samoset relished and devoured. The Pilgrims looked on in amazement. Curiosity replaced their fear, and the Pilgrims began to question the Indian of many things.

Samoset was the chief of an Abenaki tribe that resided further north of Plymouth. He and Bradford traded stories and quickly became friends—a vast contrast to the interaction between John Smith and the natives at Jamestown.

The Pilgrims also learned where all of the human bones (scattered about much of their land) derived from. Samoset told them of the tribe who had inhabited the area before their arrival until a plague wiped them all out. The Pilgrims realized that their timing in coming to America had to be God's providence.

After meeting with the Pilgrims, Samoset left the colony, only to return a week later with five other natives, who brought deerskins to trade. Among these natives was a young, energetic Indian. His name was Squanto.

> Squanto was a special instrument sent of God for our good and beyond our expectation. —William Bradford

The arrival of Squanto at Plymouth Colony would be a prime example of God's grace in their lives. He taught the Pilgrims how to grow corn, plant pumpkins, stalk deer, find berries, and catch fish. The Pilgrims had adopted him as one of their own, and he became vital to the colony's survival. It was as if all of their troubles disappeared when Squanto arrived.

But, years earlier, when Squanto had his first encounter with white men, the reception was very different. In 1605, he was kidnapped from his own home by an English explorer, Captain George Weymouth, and taken to England. Sir Ferdinando Gorges, owner of the Plymouth Company, took Squanto into his home and for the next nine years, he worked for Sir Gorges, all the while learning the English language. By 1614, Squanto found himself shipped back to America on the lower decks of a vessel, captained by none other than John Smith! Squanto was treated harshly under Smith's watch, and he attempted to escape several times, only to be caught each time. In lieu of execution, he was sent back to Europe where a group of friars eventually paid for his freedom. Under their watch, Squanto was introduced to the Book that would change his life forever – the Bible. When Squanto finally returned to the shores of America in 1619, he struggled in seeing the decimation of his entire tribe, the Patuxet, but through his newfound faith in Christ, he understood that God was not done with him yet.

With his help, the light of Christ was starting to gain the victory in Plymouth. By the fall of 1621, Bradford and the Pilgrims had a bumper crop of corn and an abounding fur trade with the Native Americans. To celebrate, the Pilgrims held a great harvest feast, and all of the nearby Native American tribes were invited.

> And God be praised we had a good increase ... Our harvest being gotten in, our governor sent four men on fowling, that

> so we might after a special manner rejoice together after we had gathered the fruit of our labors ... And although it be not always so plentiful as it was at this time with us, yet by the goodness of God, we are so far from want that we often wish you partakers of our plenty. —Edward Winslow (Pilgrim)

Before the feast began, William Brewster, minister and senior elder of the colony, led both groups in a prayer of thanks:

> Today, we thank God: for bringing us to this place; for providing all of our needs; for sustaining us, even when faith would temporarily wane; for the lives of our fellow departed – thank You for taking them home to be with You; for the opportunity to build a new home for freedom and liberty; and most of all, for our new Indian friends. For we know without them, none of this would be possible. —William Brewster

After the prayer, they ate turkey, deer, fish, lobster, vegetables, berries, pies, and, of course, cornbread—the result of a bountiful corn harvest. All day the feasting continued, and well into the evening. Between meals, the Pilgrims and Indians happily competed in shooting contests—gun and bow. The Indians were especially delighted when some of the younger Pilgrim boys were eager to join them in foot races and leg wrestling. The natives showed no inclination to leave and enjoyed themselves so much that they stayed for nearly three days! This great harvest feast led to the inspiration for what would become a cherished American tradition—Thanksgiving.

THANKSGIVING

The word evokes images of football, family reunions, turkey, and all the trimmings. But, for the Pilgrims and the Native Americans, Thanksgiving was a festival of prayer—a prayer not only of thanksgiving to God but, also, a prayer for His providence.

In fact, for believers, the Word of God reveals a longing for providence throughout the world.

"For the earnest expectation of the creature waiteth for the manifestation of the sons of God ... Because the creature itself also shall be delivered from the bondage of corruption into the glorious liberty of the children of God" (Rom. 8:19, 21).

The Pilgrims trusted in God's providence time and time again. When they entered the starving time of 1621, the Pilgrims were reduced to a daily ration of five kernels of corn apiece. Five kernels! But, they had a choice—either give in to bitterness and despair or trust in Christ. Even in their darkest hour, they chose Christ.

For the Pilgrims, Thanksgiving wasn't only about giving thanks for the abundant provisions on the table and the friendly tribesmen who joined them; it was about giving thanks to the Provider who gave them those blessings.

While many people today follow the Pilgrims' example of feasting at Thanksgiving, they too often forget or ignore the reason that the Pilgrims set aside that special day—to give thanks to God for His blessings and acknowledge their complete dependence upon Him for their existence.

One of the greatest examples of that dependence came in the summer of 1622. As the summer heat began to scorch Plymouth Colony, a drought set in, withering the corn and threatening other vital crops. The Pilgrims, along with their native companions, gathered together and earnestly prayed for the Lord to intervene in the situation.

Before day's end, clouds began to gather on the horizon and before long, a gentle rain began to fall—a gentle rain that lasted for nearly two weeks. Not being able to do anything about the weather and needing their crops to sustain them, they were completely at the mercy of God. But, He heard their ardent prayers and sent the rain.

> The rains came, without wind, or thunder or any violence and by abundant degrees it wetted the earth and soaked the crops. Within a quick period of time, the decayed corn and other fruits began to wonderfully revive. Even the Indians were astonished to behold the transformation. And afterwards all through the hot summer months, God sent seasonable showers. Through God's blessings, He caused a fruitful and liberal harvest to our comfort and rejoicing. —William Bradford

The arrival of Squanto in Plymouth wasn't only a gift to the Pilgrims, but it was a gift to Squanto himself as he began to witness the fruits of his labor. His bold example within the colony led to the signing of a peace treaty between the natives and the

Pilgrims—a historic treaty that marked not only a peaceful relationship between the two groups but, also, a pact to defend one another in battle if either was ever attacked by other tribes or marauders. The bond they shared is a strong testimony to the love of Christ that was within them all.

NOVEMBER 1622

Plymouth was alive and flourishing, but it was about to suffer one of its greatest setbacks—a death of one of their own, Squanto.

Just before he passed away, Squanto asked Bradford to pray for him.

> You speak for the Christian God in which I serve. —Squanto to Bradford

Bradford kneeled at Squanto's side and granted his request. Days later, Bradford took to his journal and reflected on the loss of his dear friend.

> Squanto fell ill ... Bleeding much at the nose, which the Indians take as a symptom of death, and within a few days he died. He begged me to pray for him, that he might go to the Englishman's God in heaven, and bequeathed several of his things to us, as remembrances. His death was a great loss. —William Bradford

When talking about the founding of the New World, it is impossible to name a more important group than the Pilgrims. They felt a calling by Christ to put the gospel into practice in the New World, creating a society of liberty and justice for all. They had counted the cost, and they knew of the pitfalls, but they were determined to overcome. During the first winter in Plymouth, the Pilgrims lost nearly half their number to sickness, but God's hand was upon them. And with the providential arrival of young Squanto, the death rate in Plymouth fell to such a low level it was unmatched by any other colony in the history of the Americas. But, it was under Bradford's leadership that the Pilgrims learned to survive—a leadership derived from his faith in God's providence.

> Thus out of small beginnings greater things have been produced by His hand yet made all things of nothing, and gives being to all things that are; and as one small candle may light a thousand, so ye light here kindled hath shone to many, yea in some sort to our whole nation; let ye glorious name of Jehovah have all the praise. —William Bradford

The Pilgrims of Plymouth Colony didn't come to America in the name of industry; they came to plant the banner of freedom in the name of Jesus Christ.

God prepared those of humble beginnings to be a light of liberty to the world. From hard experience, the Pilgrims knew that God must forever be at the center of their lives—trusting solely in Him and maintaining their faith that He would deliver them.

The Pilgrims were torchbearers on the edge of a vast and dark continent, but the light of Christ had begun to shine in the New World. Through their sacrifice, God had planted the seeds of a nation that would become the new Promised Land.

> As one small candle may light a thousand, so the light kindled here has shown unto many, in some sort to our whole nation. —William Bradford

He may not have known it then, but the nation Bradford spoke of was to be the United States of America.

Benjamin Franklin listens to George Whitefield preach in Philadelphia.

CHAPTER 3

AWAKE THOU THAT SLEEPEST

CHAPTER THREE

AWAKE THOU THAT SLEEPEST

"And the whole multitude of the people were praying without at the time of incense. And there appeared unto him an angel of the Lord standing on the right side of the altar of incense. And when Zacharias saw him, he was troubled, and fear fell upon him. But the angel said unto him, Fear not, Zacharias: for thy prayer is heard; and thy wife Elisabeth shall bear thee a son, and thou shalt call his name John. And thou shalt have joy and gladness; and many shall rejoice at his birth. For he shall be great in the sight of the Lord, and shall drink neither wine nor strong drink; and he shall be filled with the Holy Ghost, even from his mother's womb. And many of the children of Israel shall he turn to the Lord their God. And he shall go before Him in the spirit and power of Elias, to turn the hearts of the fathers to the children, and the disobedient to the wisdom of the just; to make ready a people prepared for the Lord" (Lk. 1:10-17).

Just as God raised up John the Baptist to proclaim the coming Messiah to Israel, America, too, was raised up to proclaim the gospel of Jesus Christ to the world.

Looking back at the influence of Christianity in America, we are able to pinpoint prominent eras in our history that are clear evidence of God's deliverance and providence: World War II, the Civil War, the Revolutionary War, etc. It is hard to refute God's guiding hand influencing the very heartbeat of our nation at every turn, but these are merely focal points in American history. We must look at the whole timeline so that we can clearly understand how God built His new cornerstone of liberty in the New World, generation by generation.

In our study of the Pilgrims in Chapter 2, we learned that William Bradford and the Plymouth colonists were the founding fathers to the Founding Fathers, but we have a 150-year span between the signing of the Mayflower Compact and the Declaration of Independence in 1776.

During this time, the steam engine and the piano were invented, while commodities such as rubber and steel were discovered. Global commerce exploded as more accurate world maps gave way to new and unprecedented nautical trade routes. Bach and Mozart were composing some of the most beautiful classical music in Europe as Edward Thatch, better known as *Blackbeard,* roamed the Atlantic seas with his pirate fleet.

Change also occurred in the British colonies of America. Remote and independent colonies developed from sprawling settlements into bustling cities, ripe with industry and innovation. Roadways changed from dirt paths for sparse horsemen to stone streets for horse-drawn carriages.

However, the changes were not all physical. The colonists were beginning to call themselves Americans. As 13 distinct colonies formed, American colonists were now proud to say that they were from Virginia, North Carolina, or New York. By the time we reach the generation of Washington, Adams, and Rush, most Americans were also proud to say that they were Christian.

Spiritual fervor would rise and fall throughout the colonies over the course of the 17TH century, cooling with spiritual apathy, and then awakening under the Holy Spirit's outpouring of revival. However, as the vision would fade, God would ignite the flame again and again. After all, the fire of the Holy Spirit is the only remedy for unbelief.

If we look without scrutiny at the Pilgrims, Puritans, and many of our Founding Fathers, it would seem as if those 150 years bore the fruit of faith, virtue, piety, and grace. That's not exactly true.

Yes, the Pilgrims and the Puritans came to America to create a biblically centered society – pious, prosperous communities built on the Word of God. These men and women had a sincere call on their lives, and they fully believed in what the Lord was establishing through them in the New World. But, among all of the change and transformation, generations that directly followed the Pilgrims and the Puritans were becoming complacent and apathetic. As the years passed and different generations came and went, the new Zion they were building began to erode.

Psalm 78:2-8 says: *"I will open my mouth in a parable: I will utter dark sayings of old: Which we have heard and known, and our fathers have told us. We will not hide them from their children, showing to the generation to come the praises of the Lord, and His strength, and His wonderful works that he has done. For he established a testimony in Jacob, and appointed a law in Israel, which he commanded our fathers, that they should make them known to their children. That the generation to come might know them, even the children which should be born; who should arise and declare them to their children: That they might set their hope in God, and not forget the works of God, but keep His commandments: And might not be as their fathers, a stubborn and rebellious generation; a generation that set not their heart aright, and whose spirit was not stedfast with God."*

In Massachusetts, witchcraft became the biggest point of contention in a rebellious generation. What began as an isolated incident in the quiet village of Salem quickly escalated into a wave of hysteria.

It was 1692, and Samuel Parris found himself in the center of a perilous conflict. Suspicion of demonic activity inside his home began to surface, namely from his daughter, Elizabeth Parris, his niece, Abigail Williams, and their friend, Ann Putnam, Jr. Many locals speculated that the girls were involved in witchcraft after they began displaying a great deal of unusual and demon-like behaviors in public. Speculation quickly shifted to confirmation when Samuel Parris found out the girls had been hanging out with Tituba, an Indian slave from Barbados. Tituba gained an influence in the young girls' lives and lured them into the practices of witchcraft. The story garnered the attention of the entire village, which led to an outbreak of suspicion and accusations, by the young girls, of others all over town. A special court was convened to hear each case, better known today as the "Salem Witch Trials." However, Salem's answer to combating witchcraft turned into a cloudy quandary.

The inability to memorize Scriptures or recite the Lord's Prayer became the only formula to deciding whether one was guilty or not. The holes in this logic were far too numerous to count, and many citizens were wrongfully accused.

Cotton Mather, a New England Puritan minister, penned a letter entitled, *The Return of Several Ministers Consulted*. In it, he noted that "spectral evidence" was being used in excess to indict presumed witches, meaning it was merely evidence based upon dreams and visions. Something had to be done to make sure that innocent people weren't being convicted, or even worse, put to death unjustly.

Cotton's father, Increase Mather, followed up with a book entitled, *Cases of Conscience Concerning Evil Spirits*. In it, he also acknowledged the gross overuse of spectral evidence. He argued that "it would be better that ten witches go free than the blood of a single innocent be shed."

Thanks to their influence, public opinion shifted in opposition of the trials, and every prisoner was eventually pardoned, but the damage was already done. Over the course of six months, nearly 200 men, women, and children were hung from Salem's Gallows Hill.

By the early 18TH century, true Christian living had grown cold. As people turned away from God, drunkenness and debauchery seeped into the colonies as their Bibles began to collect dust. Once peaceful communities transitioned into endless quarrels over property disputes and business dealings.

Men and women became more concerned with their own personal affairs. Money, work, and social standing took precedence in their lives.

As the people's concerns drifted from the Word of God, so did the preaching. Older generations had faced the trials that led to faith in the providence of God. Since the younger generations had never known anything but blessing, they could hardly share in the gratefulness of their parents.

Reverend Samuel Willard, a Massachusetts born minister said in 1700: "It hath been a frequent observation that if one generation begins to decline the next that followeth it usually grows worse and so on 'til God poureth out His Spirit again upon them."

People became complacent in their sin. Some perceived the gospel as inconvenient; others were outright rejecting it.

During this time of great spiritual neglect, the church looked to other means to bolster its numbers. Preachers were doing anything to keep people in their pews. "Half-way covenants" became popular—akin to the papal indulgences of old. People could literally pay to maintain their social standing. Church had become more or less a social club.

Out along the fringes of settlement, many of the colonists were unchurched. On the frontier, people simply had no minister to preach to them. Without the church, these pioneers had lapsed into a primitive and sinful life, little different from that of the "heathen" Indians.

Many call this period of time, "America's Middle Ages." The spiritual light of the Pilgrims and Puritans was fading, but as the night is darkest before the dawn, God would begin planting the seeds of light in America. He was preparing men who would awaken the hearts and minds of the colonists.

A group of dedicated and godly preachers (without whom a strong church could not stand) were being groomed by God to address the slumber of the colonial masses, sparking a spiritual resurrection in America's first Great Awakening.

One shining example was John Winthrop. While he didn't go by the title of "preacher," he was a devoted follower of Christ and a minister of the gospel. Just before the Great Migration of 1629 when more than 65,000 migrants came to the New World, Winthrop was unanimously selected to lead the newly established Massachusetts Bay Colony. They couldn't have chosen a better man. He was strong and compassionate, but most importantly, he was a man with a deeply committed relationship with the Lord. In passage to America, Winthrop wrote a sermon entitled, *A Model of Christian Charity*. In it, he spoke of his desire to build a faithful community of believers in the New World to be as a "city upon a hill."

Cotton Mather described Winthrop as the "American Nehemiah," referring to the Old Testament leader, who had brought the Israelites back from Babylonian captivity and rebuilt the walls of Jerusalem. Just as Nehemiah built the walls of Jerusalem, God used men like John Winthrop to build the foundation for His kingdom in America.

To reinforce the foundation, God called Samuel Davies. Davies wasn't only a preacher, but also a gifted educator, poet, and composer. Davies had the unique ability of combining theology, poetry, and music to reach the masses. He is remembered most for focusing his attention on the evangelization of slaves. Although controversial, he expressed genuine concerns about their spiritual well being. He felt that through the eyes of the Lord, each slave was a person just as much as anyone else with a heart and a soul.

After suffering a series of personal hardships, Davies' ministry became even more impactful. At the age of 24, he was diagnosed with tuberculosis. Only months later, his wife died from a miscarriage. From that point forward, Davies felt a sense of urgency on his calling, and he threw himself wholeheartedly into ministry. He served as the fourth president of Princeton University, all the while advocating for religious freedom and instituting significant religious reforms in the Virginia Colony.

To magnify the foundation, God called Jonathan Edwards. One of America's most brilliant philosophers and theologians, Edwards was a child prodigy, graduating from Yale as valedictorian at the age of 17, and going on to serve the Congregational church in Northampton, Massachusetts. He immediately found the town's spirituality on life support. The young people of his town were addicted to sinful pleasures, frequenting the tavern and indulging in lewd practices. Christians, he believed, had become preoccupied with making money. Religion had become too worldly, and Edwards singled out Deists as particularly despicable for having "cast off the Christian religion" by believing that "God has given mankind no other light to walk by but their own reason."

> Our people do not so much need to have their heads stored with knowledge as to have their hearts touched. —Jonathan Edwards

Edwards' stoic demeanor and calm delivery were not indicative of the powerful content that energized his congregation. His graphic descriptions of the torments of hell and his illustrations of the delights of heaven had rekindled spiritual fervor among his congregants. People began feeling the conviction of the Holy Spirit.

Before long, it was uncommon to see anyone walking the streets on a Sunday when Edwards was preaching. Hard hearts turned soft, cold hearts turned warm, and narrow minds opened to the love of God. The Holy Spirit had been rejuvenated in the hearts and lives of Edwards' congregation.

> It was no longer the Tavern that drew local crowds; but the Ministers' house. —Jonathan Edwards

Jonathan Edwards helped to breed the American spirit of optimism by showing the benevolence of God. While the United States of America did not yet exist, he foresaw a future glory for the great place in which he lived.

> God made it, I suppose, the greatest occasion of awakening to others, of anything that ever came to pass in the town. I have had abundant opportunity to know the effect it had, by my private conversation with many. The news of it

> seemed to be almost like a flash of lightning upon the hearts of young people all over the town, and upon many others. The noise of the dry bones waxed louder and louder. And the work of conversion was carried on in a most astonishing manner and increased more and more; souls did, as it were, come by flocks to Jesus Christ. This work of God, as it was carried on and the number of true saints multiplied, soon made a glorious alteration in the town, so that in the spring and summer following, the town seemed to be full of the presence of God. It never was so full of love, nor so full of joy ... There were remarkable tokens of God's presence in almost every house. It was a time of joy in families on the account of salvations being brought unto them, parents rejoicing over their children as new born, and husbands over their wives, and wives over their husbands. The congregation was alive in God's service ... Some weeping with sorrow and distress, others with joy and love, others with pity and concern for their neighbors. There were many instances of persons that came from abroad, on visits or on business, who partook of that shower of divine blessing that God rained down here and went home rejoicing. Till at length the same work began to appear and prevail in several other towns in the country ... In every place, God brought His saving blessings with Him, and His word, attended with Spirit ... Returned not void. —Jonathan Edwards

Not everyone was on board, however. Edwards was attacked mainly by other pastors who thought his style to be too offbeat from the traditions of the church. The strongest assault came from Charles Chauncey, a minister at First Church in Boston. Chauncey tried Edwards' revival approach of preaching but found himself to be far from successful, and he chastised anyone else who embraced it. He attacked Edwards for stirring up the passions of the people, but Edwards defended himself. Instead of talking about the "passions," he spoke of the "affections." Edwards saw nothing wrong with emotions in worship or reason in biblical study.

In 1741, Edwards delivered what would become his most famous sermon to a group of several thousand in Enfield, Massachusetts. Entitled *Sinners in the Hands of an Angry God,* Edwards reminded his congregation that hell is real, that God's vision is omnipotent, and his judgment certain. He noted that God "holds you over the pit of hell, much as one holds a spider, or some loathsome insect, over the fire, abhors you, and is dreadfully provoked ... He looks upon you as worthy of nothing else, but to be cast into the fire."

When Edwards finished, the congregation erupted with such zeal that he had to wait several minutes for them to quiet down before the closing hymn could be sung.

Whenever and wherever Edwards preached, spectators would often interrupt his preaching, crying and repenting to the Lord and appealing for salvation as they felt the conviction of the Holy Spirit. Edwards didn't sugarcoat the Scriptures. He was authentic with his congregation regarding the dangers of sin and the bondage it brings. He painted a graphic depiction of hell, emphasizing its certainty for the unredeemed, but by the same token, he preached the salvation of Christ's redeeming love.

To advance the foundation, God called two brothers—John and Charles Wesley—to preach in the New World, but God would deal with their hearts en route to America.

During the early stages of their voyage from Europe, they got to know a group of fellow passengers. They called themselves Moravians. One night, as the Moravians began their evening psalm singing, a fierce storm set in. Violent swells tossed the ship, ripping the mast in half and pouring water over and through the decks. The other passengers screamed, but the Moravians kept singing amid the chaos. The Wesleys were moved, witnessing their resolute faith and joy in the Lord as they braved the elements.

John Wesley befriended a Moravian pastor on the ship, who presented a number of challenging questions to Wesley. The simplest, yet most poignant of all, was, "Do you know beyond a shadow of a doubt that He has saved you?" Conviction flooded John Wesley's soul. Whatever these people had, he feared he didn't have it.

> I was strongly convinced that the cause of uneasiness was unbelief, and that gaining a true, living faith was the one thing needful for me ... A true faith in Christ ... I was quite amazed, and looked upon it as a new Gospel ... I felt my heart strangely warmed. I felt I did trust in Christ; Christ alone, for salvation; and an assurance was given me, that he had taken away my sins, even mine, and saved me from the law of sin & death. —John Wesley

John and Charles Wesley only spent a few years in America, but it was their journey to the New World that led to their fresh interpretation of the gospel and their true conversions in Christ. They fell under scrutiny, harassment, and persecution by the Church of England, but not before starting what we now know as Methodism.

The apathetic church was in the midst of a spiritual awakening, but this movement had yet to see its finest hour. Another man would step up to the plate and become the final catalyst of the first Great Awakening. His name was George Whitefield.

It was Whitefield who would cement the foundation for God's kingdom in America. Congregations were often lifeless, he claimed, because "dead men preached to them." Too many ministers were "slothful shepherds" and "dumb dogs."

The first Great Awakening was a turning point for the people of the American colonies. It was a turning point that drove the church to decide: Be of this world or build a nation based solely on God's Word. Could the dream of a land where one could worship God openly and freely really exist? Was it worth fighting for? Would it give birth to a new nation? Men like Jonathan Edwards provided the spark. The Wesley brothers spread the flames. However, it was Whitefield who would engulf American congregations into an inferno of righteous revival.

Born in Gloucester, England, in 1714, George Whitefield was an exuberant and devout young man who came to America with one mission—to preach the gospel of Jesus Christ.

Oxford educated at the same time as the Wesleys, Whitefield was taught early in his life to put emphasis on a well-disciplined spiritual life, but this discipline of faith was in works and works alone.

He joined The Holy Club at the university, which was founded by the Wesleys, but none of them realized they were merely Christians in name only. The Wesleys stayed complacent, but Whitefield was on fire.

In his quest for a closer relationship with Christ, Whitefield threw himself into an extensive study of the Word and was baffled to discover that all of his good works meant nothing. This realization shook him to the core. He realized all a sinner needed to do was ask for the Lord's forgiveness and accept Christ into his heart! Whitefield severed ties with the Wesley brothers, who had yet to see the light at the time, but at last, Whitefield was truly transformed; he was born again.

From that point forward, the Wesley brothers and George Whitefield were cordial, but theologically, they rarely saw eye-to-eye. In fact, at Whitefield's funeral, John Wesley spoke of his devotion and friendship with the famous preacher, saying how much he had cherished their time as brothers in Christ, but concerning some points, they had "agreed to disagree." Wesley thanked God for placing Whitefield in his life, however, and recounted that he had given his first open field sermon with Whitefield. A younger John Wesley would have considered preaching outside the walls of the church as heresy per Anglican church doctrine, but after watching Whitefield preach to farmers and their families across the fields of America, John Wesley decided to give it a try. He stepped onto a tree stump and addressed a weary group of miners after a long day of work.

John Wesley stepped onto that stump an Anglican minister, but after his sermon, he stepped back down as a preacher of the gospel. From then on, he traveled on horseback from town to town, preaching three, sometimes four, sermons a day. He didn't care if they were sinners or saved. From the stable-house to the statehouse, he would preach wherever and to whomever would listen.

Having inspired John Wesley to preach his first open-air sermon to the miners, God had used George Whitefield to start a fire that carried all the way back to England, but God's calling was for Whitefield to stay in America and add his own fuel to the flames of the first Great Awakening.

> I dare to trust that my preaching might help create one nation under God – 13 scattered colonies united with each other. —George Whitefield

In many ways, Whitefield picked up where John Wesley had left off.

> What the good Mr. John Wesley has done in America is inexpressible. His name is very precious among the people, and he has laid a foundation that I hope neither men nor devils will ever be able to shake. —George Whitefield

He was just as interested in the idea of righteousness, but he offered an added ingredient – spiritual rebirth. Wesley's message was heavy on law; Whitefield's on grace.

> Never rest until you can say 'the Lord our righteousness.' Who knows but the Lord may have mercy, nay, abundantly pardon you? Beg of God to give you faith; and if the Lord give you that, you will by it receive Christ, with his righteousness, and his all ... None, none can tell, but those happy souls who have experienced it with what demonstration of the Spirit this conviction comes ... Oh, how amiable, as well as all sufficient, does the blessed Jesus now appear! With what new eyes does the soul now see the Lord its righteousness! Brethren, it is unutterable ... Those who live godly in Christ, may not so much be said to live, as Christ to live in them ... They are led by the Spirit as a child is led by the hand of its father ... They hear, know, and obey his voice ... Being born again in God they habitually live to, and daily walk with God. Would you have peace with God? Away then, to God through Jesus Christ, who has purchased peace; the Lord Jesus has shed his heart's blood for this. He died for this; he rose again for this; he ascended into the highest heaven, and is now interceding at the right hand of God. —George Whitefield

Traveling from town to town, Whitefield electrified audiences with his golden voice, fiery flamboyant style, and unparalleled eloquence. Not one colonist had ever seen anything like these revivals. They gathered by the hundreds to hear him speak. The attentive congregations wept as tears streamed from their eyes.

The crowds only grew from there. From Rhode Island to Massachusetts and from Connecticut to New York, people were coming in droves to hear him preach.

To congregations accustomed to sermons strictly read from closely-written manuscripts, the free-flowing eloquence of this young, impassioned orator had great appeal to his audiences. His sermons were simple, logical, emotional, and mostly improvised. He appealed to a wide variety of people from all walks of life, urging his listeners to experience a new birth in the salvation of Jesus Christ.

> I am persuaded that the generality of preachers talk of an unknown and unfelt Christ. The reason why congregations have been so dead is because they had dead men preaching to them. How can dead men beget living children?
> —George Whitefield

Soon, he was preaching to thousands. Even Benjamin Franklin, who attended one of Whitefield's crusades on a stop in Philadelphia, was so carried away that he emptied his pockets into the collection plate. Whitefield had to stand elevated atop the courthouse steps and yell to carry his message to the massive crowd. Retracing his steps backward down Market Street until he could no longer hear Whitefield, Franklin surmised that more than 30,000 people could hear Whitefield's words! He was amazed at the carrying power of this man's voice. Of course, this took quite the physical toll on Whitefield, as he would sometimes preach until he could no longer speak.

> (Whitefield) had a loud and clear voice, and articulated his words so perfectly that he might be heard and understood

> at a great distance, especially as his auditories observed the most perfect silence ... By hearing him often, I came to distinguish easily between sermons newly composed and those which he had often preached in the course of his travels. His delivery of the latter was so improved by frequent repetition, that every accent, every emphasis, every modulation of the voice, was so perfectly well tuned and well placed that, without being interested in the subject, one could not help being pleased with the discourse. —Benjamin Franklin

Franklin was appreciative of Whitefield's ministry and made no hesitation at befriending this fiery, English minister. Franklin printed many of Whitefield's sermons and journals at no cost. He even built a grand auditorium in Philadelphia for the sole purpose of accommodating Whitefield's sermons.

> It was wonderful to see the change soon made in the manners of our inhabitants. From being thoughtless or indifferent about religion, it seemed as if all the world were growing spiritual, so that one could not walk thro' the town in an evening without hearing psalms sung in different families of every street. —Benjamin Franklin

As goes the church, so goes the nation. George Whitefield understood that it wasn't enough to associate with the Bible every once in awhile or go to church once a week. To him, the Cross must always be at the center of our lives, not only for our sake but also for the spiritual livelihood of our children.

Whitefield won the hearts of all people, young and old alike. Run-down churches began to flourish once more, and new ones blossomed wherever he went.

But, the more he preached, the more his health declined. Friends would beg him to stay in bed, but he would have none of it. During his final year of ministry, he still preached hundreds of times, riding through the backwoods of New England, covering nearly 2,000 miles in less than 6 months. It's a miracle that he felt as healthy as he did because preaching two, three, sometimes four times a day, an hour or two per sermon, is a brutal schedule physically, emotionally, mentally, and vocally. It is clear to see that Whitefield was a man after God's own heart. He had cheerfully elected to go the way of the Cross, and he counted it nothing but gain to have the privilege of taking it up daily.

Like Christ, he set his face toward Jerusalem. It's estimated that in his lifetime, nearly 80 percent of the colonists heard Whitefield preach at least once, and the power of the Holy Spirit fell everywhere he preached. Through the ministry of this man, the Lord was uniting the 13 Colonies on a level so deep that few people even realized what was happening. But, wherever Whitefield went, he was preaching the true gospel—the gospel of Jesus Christ.

New England Puritanism disintegrated amid the revivals. The Puritan ideal of religious uniformity was shattered, but the Protestant wing of Christianity constantly gave birth to new movements: Methodists, Baptists, Quakers, and Unitarians, sometimes referred to as 'Dissenters.' Their foundations were established throughout the 18TH century.

Preachers like Jonathan Edwards, John Wesley, and George Whitefield inspired many imitators, but in many ways, it backfired. Some of them carried evangelism to dangerous extremes, and once unleashed, it became hard to control. Reverend James Davenport, a fiery New England Congregationalist, set about shouting, raging, and stomping on the devil, beseeching his listeners to renounce the established clergy and become the agents of their own salvation. Hundreds would show up to see his theatrical sermons. Seized by terror, they groveled on the floor or lay unconscious in their chairs—charged by devilish delusions—intending to discredit the true faith.

Established clergy resented men like Edwards and Whitefield for undercutting their work during the first Great Awakening. Other critics reprimanded them for being "too emotional." Some were even concerned that evangelicals were encouraging women to speak at revivals, reminding congregations of the scriptural commandment to *"let your women keep silence in the churches."*

Irrespective, critics' words seemed to have no diminishing effect on the numbers of people who flocked to hear these men preach. They generated an unprecedented excitement among the colonists, notably in the African-American community. In fact, George Whitefield was the first minister to include black men and women in his meetings, so it is no surprise that some call him the, "Father of African-American Christianity in America."

By 1750, the Great Awakening had subsided, but evangelism and revival had been forever implanted within the

American culture, arousing hopes that America would become the new Promised Land. Entire communities were giving their hearts to Christ! Hundreds of thousands of lives were changed, permanently affecting the social and moral fabric of America's society. Igniting at its base, a spiritual blaze was forever flamed by the body of Christ with each passing generation. It is a hunger so deeply engrained in the American national psyche that it can never die. It can go to sleep and lie dormant for years, but God reawakened that desire with the first Great Awakening; and what He reawakened once, He can reawaken again.

George Whitefield prayed that these colonies would unite as "one nation under God," and, fortunately, revival had united these colonies just in time. After all, the Great Awakening didn't just affect the spiritual landscape of the colonies; it altered the political landscape, as well. The same message that caused men, women, and children to draw closer to Christ also generated a natural yearning for liberty—a yearning for independence.

Colonists were becoming aware of themselves as a people—as Americans. Through this shared experience of the first Great Awakening, these scattered 13 Colonies were rediscovering God's plan to join them together by His Spirit in the common cause of advancing His kingdom. They began to see themselves as God saw them—as a people chosen by Him for a specific purpose—to be not only *"a city upon a hill,"* but a veritable fortress of light in a darkened world. However, could they trust in God enough to escape the claws of tyranny and despotism of the king of England?

Jonathan Edwards said that God had chosen America as "the glorious renovator of the world." Indeed, God sent the first Great Awakening to America to revive His people. He placed His hand on the Thirteen Colonies, and providence united them. The pursuit of liberty was not a voice crying out of the depth of the dark past, but it was a product of the enlightened present, setting its face steadfast toward the future.

Benjamin Franklin, John Adams, and Thomas Jefferson draft the Declaration of Independence.

CHAPTER 4

PROCLAIM LIBERTY

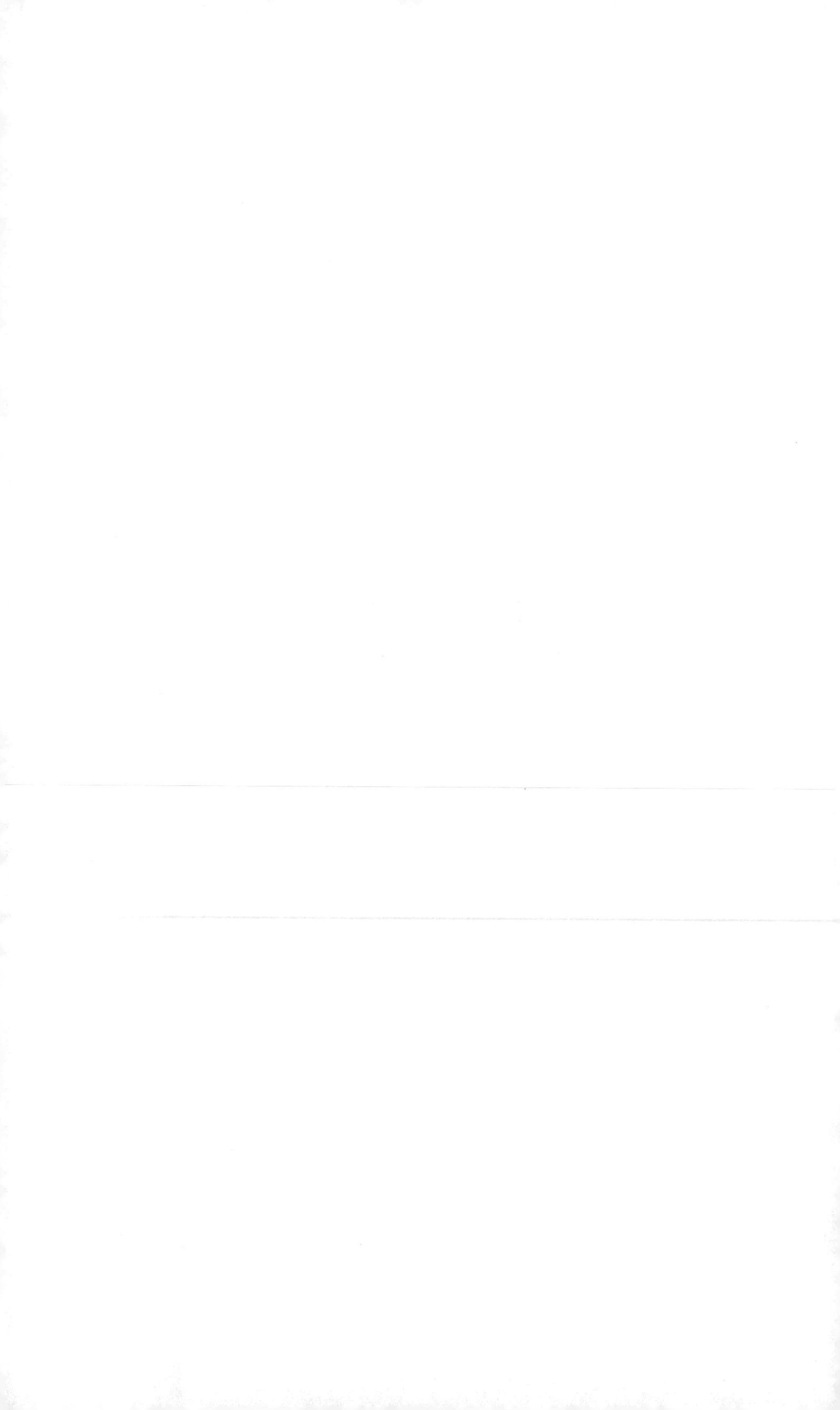

CHAPTER FOUR

PROCLAIM LIBERTY

The Declaration of Independence is often thought of as the document that started the American Revolution, but, in all reality, the Declaration of Independence, penned by America's Founding Fathers, was not the cause, but rather the effect of the revolution.

> When in the Course of human events, it becomes necessary for one people to dissolve the political bands which have connected them with another, and to assume among the powers of the earth, the separate and equal station to which the Laws of Nature and of Nature's God entitle them, a decent respect to the opinions of mankind requires that they should declare the causes which impel them to the separation. —Declaration of Independence

When it comes to the American Revolution, we often think of the bloody war of attrition fought by colonists with muskets and cannons, but the revolution, we *should* remember, happened far before Thomas Jefferson ever put pen to paper. The real American Revolution took place in the hearts and minds of colonists as they began to understand that certain rights, granted by God, were universal and applied to all men, not a select few. And these sacred and undeniable rights came from a higher power, which superseded king and country alike, and the right to life and the liberty to live that life in pursuit of happiness was available to every living being by the Creator of heaven and earth.

This revolutionary idea was unheard of. A nation based on the natural rights of all citizens? Kings, princes, and potentates were all the Western world knew of governmental authority. emperors, caesars, sultans, czars - no matter what title was given, they were *the* accepted rulers of a nation's subjects, divinely appointed by God to act as lord of the law. To question or disobey their rulings and directives was not only met with harsh punishment, but in the eyes of the church, it was heresy and sacrilege. The reign of despotic monarchies and oppressive religious dictators, however, was about to be shaken to its core.

Following the Seven Years' War between Great Britain and France, there were two primary objectives of King George III and parliament regarding the American colonies: To recoup the costs of the war through taxation and to guard, govern, and police the colonies with British troops. Each of these initiatives came at a great cost to both the economy and the liberty of American colonists. Through unilateral actions and executive orders, King George III passed a series of taxes, known as "Acts," upon the colonies - such taxes like the Stamp Act and the Sugar Act. But, the colonies had no representation in parliament;

therefore, there was no official channel to contest these taxes. So, the colonists protested.

Despite calls for equal representation in parliament, or at least a voice in crafting these confiscatory policies, there was no response from King George III. The silence grew deafening as the taxes grew in both number and scope. Protests—organized and otherwise—became the norm as more colonists began to feel distanced from the British Empire, to whom they were still in subjection. "Taxation without representation" became the mantra of many, who were now beginning to think of themselves as Americans instead of English subjects. There were still a great many loyalists who backed the Crown, but their numbers dwindled as the taxes grew more oppressive, and the tactics used to maintain order grew more violent.

Tensions between British soldiers and the colonists were at fever pitch. Adding to the animosity was the forced housing of some British soldiers in the colonists' homes and additional taxes to house and feed the others. The colonies were a powder keg ready to explode. It wasn't a matter of *if* but *when.*

The *when* came on March 5, 1770. Out of nowhere, British troops inflicted a barrage of musket fire on a group of civilian protestors, killing five. You may better know this incident as the Boston Massacre. Among the murdered: A black freeman, Crispus Attucks, widely considered to be the first American casualty in the American Revolution. As news spread throughout the colonies, outrage soon followed.

A group of activists, known as the Sons of Liberty, and their leaders, Samuel Adams and Paul Revere, called for action.

Twelve British (eight soldiers and four civilians) were indicted for murder. Pamphlets were circulated throughout the colonies, bringing news of the indictment and outlining the trial's proceedings. Also included with each pamphlet: A painting by Paul Revere. The depiction showed a hard line of lobsterbacks—a term coined by British soldiers because of their red-coated uniforms—firing in unison into an unarmed crowd of colonists. But, things were not as it was depicted in the painting. The crowd that assembled around the British soldiers threw rocks and brandished billy clubs, taunting the soldiers, "Fire! Fire you fools!"

A thrown object struck a young British soldier, knocking him to the ground as he lost grip of his musket. Picking it up from the ground, he shouted, "Damn you! Fire!" And it did. The first shot of the American Revolution had been fired.

As the confused British soldiers began to sporadically fire without orders, British Captain Thomas Preston shouted for cease-fire, but the damage had already been done. As the smoke cleared, six Americans lay wounded, five dead. Now, 12 British men found themselves on trial for cold-blooded murder.

But, who would defend these men? After several requests to loyalist lawyers were denied, Captain Preston sent a request to John Adams—a known patriot and cousin to Samuel Adams—pleading for him to take the case. Going against public sentiment, Adams took the case, if anything, to ensure a fair and balanced trial.

John Adams was known as a fierce litigator before the trial, but he was risking his career by defending this group of British men. Nevertheless, Adams' tenacity slowly put the pieces together and solved the puzzle of what happened the night of March 5, 1770. The aggressive riot tactics of the crowd were brought to light; the taunting threats and thrown debris were accounted for.

> Look beyond the fact that these men are British! If these soldiers were endangered by this mob, this motley rabble of saucy boys and jack tars, if they were provoked and not endangered ... They are at most guilty of manslaughter!
> —John Adams

After nearly three hours of deliberation, six of the eight soldiers were acquitted. Two were charged with manslaughter. Although this verdict showed the allegiance that future President John Adams held toward respecting the law, the colonists' mindset had already been changed.

For those promoting American independence, the Boston Massacre was seen as a golden opportunity. The growing rift between colonists and King George III only widened. Of the incident, John Adams wrote, "The foundation of American independence has been laid." The seeds of revolution were sown.

Only three years later, the British throne administered a brand new tax - the Tea Act. American colonists were furious, but the Sons of Liberty devised a plan to protest the Tea Act while also destroying an entire shipment of imported tea.

Demonstrators donned the disguises of Native Americans, hijacked all of the incoming cargo ships from the East India Trading Company, and threw all of the containers of tea overboard into the Boston Harbor. The dramatic nature of this protest—better known as the Boston Tea Party—ensured that it reached as many eyes and ears as possible, thus galvanizing the resistance movement and provoking a response from England.

King George III took notice, and he wasn't happy. He responded by passing the Coercive Acts of 1774, which essentially turned Massachusetts into a de facto police state, governed by martial law.

In response to the subjugation of Massachusetts, the First Continental Congress convened in Philadelphia to officially petition King George III with a set of grievances. First among them: The return of power to Massachusetts. Second: A reasonable reconciliation between the American colonies and Britain. The plan was to attempt a peaceful compromise at first and then reconvene if the grievances weren't addressed. At the time, they weren't even entertaining a strategy to separate from Britain. It was merely a last-ditch effort to act with diplomacy. Still, not everyone was on the same page.

The colonies were in disarray. Brother pitted against brother; American liberty versus British loyalty. But politics aside, of the 55 delegates present at the First Continental Congress, 51 were Christians. And though they may have disagreed on how to deal with the Crown, they agreed on how to kneel at the Cross. At the convention, Reverend Jacob Duché was asked to pray over the assembly:

> Be Thou present, O God of Wisdom, and direct the counsel of this Honorable Assembly; enable them to settle all things on the best and surest foundations; that the scene

> of blood may be speedily closed; that Order, Harmony and Peace may be effectually restored, and that Truth and Justice, Religion and Piety, prevail and flourish among the people. Preserve the health of their bodies and the vigor of their minds, shower down on them, and the millions they here represent, such temporal Blessings as Thou seest expedient for them in this world, and crown them with everlasting Glory in the world to come. All this we ask in the name and through the merits of Jesus Christ, Thy Son and our Saviour, Amen —Reverend Jacob Duché

Following his prayer, a calming semblance of unity settled among the delegates in Philadelphia. As they waited for a response from King George III, events were already transpiring across the Atlantic in parliament, where many Englishmen actually defended the American colonies' right to protest.

One of these men was Edmund Burke, who spoke of the colonists as brethren rather than children, as King George III often did. As an elected official of parliament, he declared that Britain should resolve the conflict in America peacefully, laying out a six-point plan to his fellow countrymen:

1. Allow the American colonists to elect their own representatives, thus settling the dispute about taxation without representation.

2. Acknowledge this wrongdoing and apologize for grievances caused.

3. Procure an efficient manner of choosing and sending these delegates.

4. Set up a general assembly in America itself, with powers to regulate taxes.

5. Stop gathering taxes by imposition (or law) and start gathering them only when they are needed.

6. Grant needed aid to the colonies.

Burke's proposal was defeated by a vote of 210 to 105, but even in its defeat, a telling story was beginning to unfold: One-third of British representatives were supportive of the American colonies and their objections. They saw the colonists' outrage not so much at the entirety of England, but at the brutality of an unruly king.

The delegates continued to patiently await a response from King George III, but before the Second Continental Congress was able to assemble, events developed that would force their hand, modifying a final attempt to compromise into an ultimatum of rebellion and war. A pamphlet had begun to circulate around the colonies, and its popularity only picked up steam with each passing minute of the king's cold-shoulder. The writer of this pamphlet was Thomas Paine and his publication was entitled *Common Sense.*

Hoping to capture the hearts of his fellow colonists, Thomas Paine presented a simple, common sense approach for freedom and independence. Written in a clear, concise language that even the common man could understand, Paine constructed a point-by-point argument for American independence, free from the grasp of British rule. And guess what? He wasn't a Christian. Even the unbelievers were onboard.

Many of the modern 'experts' who rely on Thomas Paine to be the torch-bearer for their position that this country was not founded on the Word of God would be surprised to hear some of his writings:

> The cause of America is in a great measure the cause of all mankind. Where, say some, is the king of America? I'll tell you, friend, He reigns above. Yet, that we may not appear to be defective even in earthly honors, let a day be solemnly set apart for proclaiming the charter; let it be placed on the Divine Law, the Word of God; let a crown be placed thereon. The Almighty implanted in us these inextinguishable feelings for good and wise purposes. —Excerpt from Thomas Paine's *Common Sense*

Yes, it would be untrue to say that all of America's Founding Fathers were Christians. Some of the most influential minds (such as Thomas Paine) did not claim to be, but although we can never truly know what lies in another man's heart, we can listen to what he says and watch what he does as a reflection of his faith. All of these men, even the unsaved among them, understood that Christianity was the fabric from which the American tapestry would be formed.

Common Sense was the encapsulation of the colonists' petition for freedom. Paine acquired the help of Dr. Benjamin Rush, another like-minded patriot who was well versed in natural rights. While many of the points were not revolutionary in and of themselves, Thomas Paine and Dr. Rush's simple message and straightforward style were easily printable in mass quantities, and it spread like wildfire throughout the colonies.

The appealing elements of *Common Sense* would inspire the writers of the Declaration of Independence to utilize the groundswell of support the pamphlet received. But, before they could sit down and put pen to paper, Americans would have to stand up and fight.

By the spring of 1775, the gears of war were in motion. Great Britain planned an assault on the cities of Lexington and Concord in Massachusetts. Major General Joseph Warren of the colonial patriot militia caught wind of their plan and sent Paul Revere to warn fellow militia that the British were coming. The militia—known as the Minutemen because they could be ready in a minute's notice—quickly prepared for battle.

In Lexington, more than 700 British troops marched boldly into the middle of town square. They came face to face with roughly 200 American militia. As they met, a British officer screamed, "Lay down your arms and disperse!" Captain John Parker of the militia told his boys, "Stand your ground; don't fire unless fired upon, but if they mean to have war, let it begin here!"

A shot was fired, and then another, and then another. Soon, a barrage of gunfire was being sprayed from musket to musket.

Historical accounts don't agree on who took the first shot, an American or a Brit, but what is known is that eight American colonists lost their lives in the brief gun battle. Only one British soldier was wounded. The remaining Minutemen retreated in a panic. British troops marched onward.

In his poem, "Paul Revere's Ride," Henry Wadsworth Longfellow recounted the Battle of Lexington:

... For, borne on the night-wind of the past,
Through all our history, to the last,
In the hour of darkness and peril and need,
The people will waken and listen to hear
The hurrying hoof-beats of that steed,
And the midnight message of Paul Revere.

British troops then descended on Concord, where they were charged with disarming the town militia and confiscating any war supplies.

The nearly 250 Minutemen of Concord received news that shots had been fired in Lexington and that several colonists had been killed. They didn't want to meet the same fate. Outgunned and outmanned, they chose to take the high ground outside of town to monitor British troop movements and wait for reinforcements of their own. Patience paid off.

British troops spread out to inspect the city, leaving only 100 men to guard the north bridge entrance to Concord. Out of nowhere, 400 Minutemen descended on the light infantry company. The British were dumbfounded, and this time, it was *they* who lost men—three killed and nine wounded. The skirmish ended in a mutual ceasefire, but neither side moved. For nearly 10 minutes, the Minutemen, bold and confident, stood rifle ready, staring down their English foes on the other side of the bridge. Finally, the British troops broke, retreating from the city. With that, the first battle of the Revolutionary War was over.

In his poem, "Concord Hymn," Ralph Waldo Emerson recounted the Battle of Concord:

By the rude bridge that arched the flood,
Their flag to April's breeze unfurled,
Here once the embattled farmers stood,
And fired the shot heard round the world.
The foe long since in silence slept;
Alike the conqueror silent sleeps;
And time the ruined bridge has swept
Down the dark stream which seaward creeps.
On this green bank, by this soft stream,
We set to-day a votive stone;
That memory may their deed redeem,
When, like our sires, our sons are gone.
Spirit, that made those heroes dare,
To die, and leave their children free,
Bid time and nature gently spare
The shaft we raise to them and thee.

After Lexington and Concord, there was no turning back. As John Adams put it, "The die was cast, the Rubicon crossed."

The American militia was able to muster enough support for a small victory, but the British still controlled Boston.

JUNE 17, 1775: THE BATTLE OF BUNKER HILL

Militiamen from Rhode Island, Connecticut, and New Hampshire joined in the siege as American and British forces increased in and around Boston. On the day before the battle, American forces fortified the high ground overlooking Boston. The rebels were hungry for a fight.

> The British say we won't fight; by heavens, I hope I shall die up to my knees in blood! —Joseph Warren

With civilians looking on from rooftops and church steeples, the British attacked in the blistering heat, with 2,400 troops moving in tight formation through the tall grass. Militiamen, being pounded by naval guns, watched as the waves of British troops advanced up the hill. They waited until their attackers had come within yards and then loosed a shattering assault of their own. Civilians cheered as they watched British soldiers retreat in a panic.

The British re-formed their lines and attacked again, but another barrage of gunfire from militiamen sent the vaunted redcoats running for a second time. Still, the proud British, led by General William Howe, were determined not to let the ragtag rustics humiliate them.

On the third attempt, the British finally gained some ground. Running low on gunpowder, the ill-supplied militiamen resorted to throwing stones to counter the British bayonet charge. The British took the high ground, but at the cost of more than a thousand casualties. Every one of General Howe's aides had been wounded or killed. He quickly realized that the Americans were not only there to fight, they were there to win.

JUNE 23, 1775

Nearly 300 miles away from Boston, in Philadelphia Pennsylvania, amidst all of the turmoil, a man by the name of George Washington penned a letter to his dear wife, Martha:

> My Dearest,
>
> As I am within a few Minutes of leaving this City, I could not think of departing from it without dropping you a line; especially as I do not know whether it may be in my power to write again till I get to the Camp at Boston—I go fully trusting in that Providence, which has been more bountiful to me than I deserve, & in full confidence of a happy meeting with you sometime in the Fall—I have not time to add more, as I am surrounded with Company to take leave of me—I retain an unalterable affection for you, which neither time or distance can change, my best love to Jack & Nelly, & regard for the rest of the Family concludes me with the utmost truth & sincerity.
>
> Your Entire, George Washington

This letter reveals the heart of a man seldom seen in his daily correspondence. Pressed for time, he signs the letter, "Your Entire George Washington," words that display an almost subtle vulnerability within him. Maybe the horrors of impending combat directed his emotional tone. Maybe he sensed that his role in this revolution was going to be greater than he had ever imagined.

The Second Continental Congress convened in the summer of 1775 to develop a strategy, including a last effort at diplomacy with King George III.

On July 5, 1775, 48 delegates—including John Adams, Benjamin Franklin, and Thomas Jefferson—drafted the Olive Branch Petition.

> We beg leave further to assure your Majesty that notwithstanding the sufferings of your loyal colonists during the course of the present controversy, our breasts retain too tender a regard for the kingdom from which we derive our origin to request such a reconciliation as might in any manner be inconsistent with her dignity or welfare. These, related as we are to her, honor and duty, as well as inclination induce us to support and advance; and the apprehensions that now oppress our hearts with unspeakable grief, being once removed, your Majesty will find your faithful subjects on this continent ready and willing at all times, as they ever have been with their lives and fortunes to assure and maintain the rights and interests of your Majesty and of our Mother Country.

When the king received the letter several weeks later, it was met with instant ridicule.

> It is now become the part of wisdom, and (in its effects) of clemency, to put a speedy end to these disorders by the most decisive exertions. —King George III to parliament

When the Olive Branch Petition was rebuffed by the king, the Second Continental Congress answered by authorizing an attack on British troops in the walled city of Quebec in the hopes of rallying support from its French inhabitants. Colonial forces, under General Richard Montgomery, arrived outside Quebec weak, hungry, and unprepared. They could've dealt with a brief bout of exhaustion in their attempt to surprise British forces, but they were ambushed by another brutal power—smallpox.

As the deadly virus swept through their camp in the fall of '75, General Montgomery faced a trying dilemma. Most of the soldiers had signed up for short tours of duty, many of which were scheduled to expire at the end of the year. He couldn't afford to wait for the epidemic to subside. Seeing little choice but to fight, General Montgomery ordered a desperate attack on British forces in the midst of a blizzard on December 31, 1775.

The assault was a disaster. General Montgomery was killed early in the battle, and over 400 colonists were taken prisoner. The rest of the soldiers retreated to their camp outside the walls of Quebec and appealed to congress, pleading for reinforcements.

By the spring of '76, there were only 1,900 colonial soldiers left outside Quebec, and nearly half of them were infected with smallpox. Sensing their weakness, the British attacked them, resulting in a frantic retreat back to New England. The sick were left behind. Veterans of the failed campaign brought the virus home with them, spreading the epidemic to civilians and making the recruitment of new soldiers even more challenging. Men who might have risked British gunfire balked at the more terrifying thought of contracting smallpox in a military camp.

Congress continued to hold back from declaring independence. Yet, as the months passed, word came of one British action after another that gradually demoralized the already grief-stricken colonists. When British forces conquered and assumed control over the port of Boston, it left congress with only one option: a declaration of war.

> These United Colonies are, and of right ought to be, free and independent states. —Richard Henry Lee

> There is a tide in the affairs of men. We perceive it now before us. To hesitate is to consent to our own slavery ... Though these gray hairs must soon descend to the grave, I would infinitely rather that they descend there by the hand of the executioner than desert at the crisis the sacred cause of my country. —Reverend John Witherspoon

> His majesty can now read my name without glasses. And he can also double the price of my head. We must be unanimous; there must be no pulling different ways; we must all hang together. —John Hancock

> We have this day restored the Sovereign to Whom alone men ought to be obedient. He reigns in heaven and ... From the rising to the setting sun, may His kingdom come.
> —Samuel Adams

Samuel Adams is called the father of the American Revolution because he understood that the conflict between the British government and the American colonies was more than just an economic or political struggle. It was a battle for freedom and liberty in the name of Christianity. The first Great Awakening generated a spirit of faith, confidence, and liberty within the colonists. They knew that they were inherently free and could no longer bow to the despotism of the Crown. But, in order for independence to be realized, Samuel Adams knew that his convictions would have to be heralded as one voice throughout the colonies.

Congress began functioning as the de facto government of the 13 Colonies—issuing currency, broadening foreign relations, developing intelligence, and organizing tenderfoot militias into a capable army. And its army needed a relentless leader that would not only inspire, but also bring the strategy and experience that they would need to face the world's greatest military power—a leader that would usher America's cause as a radiant beacon of liberty for generations to come. That leader would be George Washington.

The Second Continental Congress now faced the daunting task of building a case for war against Britain.

"We hold these truths to be self-evident, that all men are created equal, that they are endowed by their Creator with certain

unalienable Rights, that among these are Life, Liberty and the pursuit of Happiness."

A case based on Judeo-Christian values.

"We, therefore, the Representatives of the united States of America, in General Congress, Assembled, appealing to the Supreme Judge of the world for the rectitude of our intentions, do, in the Name, and by Authority of the good People of these Colonies, solemnly publish and declare ... "

A case to form an objectively ruled republic against the will of the British Empire.

"... That these United Colonies are, and of Right ought to be Free and Independent States; that they are Absolved from all Allegiance to the British Crown, and that all political connection between them and the State of Great Britain, is and ought to be totally dissolved; and that as Free and Independent States, they have full Power to levy War, conclude Peace, contract Alliances, establish Commerce, and to do all other Acts and Things which Independent States may of right do ... "

A case that would overthrow the basic notions of thousands of years of tradition.

"... And for the support of this Declaration, with a firm reliance on the protection of divine Providence, we mutually pledge to each other our Lives, our Fortunes and our sacred Honor."

A case that required a declaration—a declaration of independence.

One by one, each colony authorized its congressional delegates to endorse the final step towards independence.

The resolution passed on July 2, 1776.

The next day, John Adams wrote to his wife, Abigail:

> I am well aware of the Toil and Blood and Treasure, that it will cost us to maintain this Declaration, and support and defend these States. Yet through all the Gloom I can see the Rays of ravishing Light and Glory. I can see that the End is more than worth all the Means. And that Posterity will triumph in that Day's Transaction, even although we should rue it, which I trust in God we shall not.

On July 4, 1776, after days of writing and countless drafts, Thomas Jefferson submitted the formal Declaration of Independence to be voted on by Congress.

> This was the object of the Declaration of Independence. Not to find out new principles, or new arguments, never before thought of, not merely to say things which had never been said before; but to place before mankind the common sense of the subject, in terms so plain and firm as to command their assent, and to justify ourselves in the independent stand we are compelled to take. Neither aiming at originality of principle or sentiment, nor yet copied from any particular and previous writing, it was intended to be an expression of the American mind, and to give to that expression the proper tone and spirit called for by the occasion.
> —Thomas Jefferson

The motion passed unanimously.

After the announcement of the vote, silence moved over the delegates as they contemplated the magnitude of what they had just done. Some wept openly, while others bowed in prayer. They were no longer subjects. They were no longer colonists. Now, they were Americans.

The Declaration of Independence, therein, became a proclamation of faith. It was a letter to the newly crowned American citizens letting them know that sovereignty had been transferred from the tyranny of King George III and given to the citizenry.

> It is a common observation here that our cause is the cause of all mankind, and that we are fighting for their liberty in defending our own. —Benjamin Franklin

Our Founding Fathers adhered to such a firm reliance upon God, they insisted their biblical convictions be included in the Declaration of Independence. Thus, the phrases, "endowed by their Creator," "appealing to the Supreme Judge of the World," and "with a firm reliance on the protection of Divine providence," were added to the final draft of this document. It reflects not only our founders' faith in God, but also sheds light on the biblical principles that had been sown into the hearts of American colonists for more than 150 years, namely, through the first Great Awakening.

Beyond uniting the colonies against a common enemy, the Declaration of Independence was a broad acknowledgment of the divinely granted rights of mankind. Anger over the inequalities enforced by an oppressive monarchy, the colonists' ideals of independence and desire for self-government were anchored by the belief in underlying principles—the principles of natural law. English philosopher and enlightenment writer, John Locke, advocated the notion of natural law and, in turn, the natural rights of man. A Christian himself, Locke was a great inspiration to the Founding Fathers, and more specifically, the three men who helped to craft the Declaration of Independence—Thomas Jefferson, Benjamin Franklin, and John Adams.

The fundamental assertions of Locke's political theory served as the foundation for the most basic concepts of the Declaration; chief among them were equality, the right to life and liberty, and the freedom to pursue happiness. Locke believed that men, in their natural state, were all equal and independent and endowed by God with natural rights to defend life, liberty, and property. This idea of natural rights cast aside the old world notion of the "divine right of kings," challenged the conventions of imperial monarchy, and defied the very idea of kingship itself. Equality of *all* men meant that *no one*—not even royalty—was above God's natural law.

This was not only revolutionary thinking, but for England and the king, it was treasonous. The very idea of a king as merely a man was in itself sacrilege. It was considered heresy to speak against, much less take action against, the Crown. To challenge the false foundations of divine power on which monarchies were built would redefine not only the direct relationship between man and government but also between man and God.

Monarchs had succeeded for centuries in subduing others—namely Christians—by taking certain Scriptures from the Word of God out of context and pinpointing them to ratify their sovereignty. Some nations justified their sovereignty through biblical authority by claiming that the king or queen's lineage traced back to Adam and Eve, professing heritage as their reasoning for ruling the people as God's will. America was ready to challenge all of that.

The stage was now set for armed conflict between Great Britain and the new American nation. There was still a reluctance to jump into a war that seemed nearly impossible to win, what with a disorganized and largely untrained militia made up of farmers and citizen soldiers, no significant Navy, no money or established supply lines, and, of course, no officially organized national government to speak of. But, it was imperative that they unite to have any chance at victory.

> We must all hang together, or assuredly we shall all hang separately. —Benjamin Franklin

There was no turning back now.

> With hearts fortified with these animating reflections, we most solemnly, before God and the world, declare, that, exerting the utmost energy of those powers, which our beneficent Creator hath graciously bestowed upon us, the arms we have compelled by our enemies to assume, we will, in defiance of every hazard, with unabating firmness and perseverance employ for the preservation of our liberties; being with one mind resolved to die freemen rather than to live as slaves. —Thomas Jefferson

Americans may look back now and feel the warmth and proudness of its heritage, but the reality that Americans woke up to on July 5, 1776, was a little more unsettling. Their oath, "For king and country ... To be faithful to the king and bear true allegiance to the king, so help me God," was now null and void. No king, no religion, no state church held the leash of liberty any longer. They were on their own. They had gone from being disgruntled subjects of the most powerful empire on earth to citizens of a rogue nation. And now, they prepared for war.

George Washington reads the Declaration of Independence to his troops.

CHAPTER 5

FOR SUCH A TIME AS THIS

CHAPTER FIVE

FOR SUCH A TIME AS THIS

"America is another name for opportunity. Our whole history appears like a last effort of divine providence on behalf of the human race." —Ralph Waldo Emerson

So, it had come to this: Thirteen years after Great Britain acquired supremacy in North America with the Treaty of Paris in 1763, American patriots were now willing to fight for their freedom against the most formidable military power of its time.

The signing of the Declaration of Independence generated excitement among the newly crowned Americans. Yet, while it was one thing for them to declare independence from British authority on paper, it was quite another for them to earn that independence on the battlefield. All odds favored the British, and King George III wasted no time recruiting mercenaries in Europe to assist Great Britain. With nearly 30,000 Germans sailing to America's shores under the English flag, George

Washington found himself in command of a poorly supplied, inexperienced army.

JULY 9, 1776

Only days after the Second Continental Congress voted for independence, a vanguard of British redcoats was landing on undefended soil in Staten Island, New York. It was the first wave of a monumental British effort to stun and subdue the rebellious Americans.

Just a few miles away, thousands of Continental soldiers gathered at the steps of city hall in Lower Manhattan. Many had traveled from Boston to defend New York City from the advancing British and were awaiting word from their commander-in-chief, General George Washington—that word being the newly adopted Declaration of Independence. Washington prayed that this statement of faith would serve as a boost of encouragement for his young, emaciated soldiers. Although ill-supplied and under-prepared, Washington knew he had a greater power on his side ... Providence.

Washington had the stature of a leader. He was tall and strong, a superb horseman, and a fearless fighter. He had so much martial dignity in his appearance, you could distinguish him as a general from among a thousand men. The Continental Congress had fastened on him by virtue of his service in a previous war, making him one of the most experienced officers in America.

More than 20 years prior, in the midst of the French and Indian War, British General Edward Braddock arrived from England with two regiments of troops. His job was to drive out French forces camped along the Ohio Valley territory. When he arrived, he heard stories of a young American officer whom he sought to recruit for his staff. This was a 23-year-old George Washington. Washington joined General Braddock and his band of troops, and they marched for weeks toward the French-occupied Fort Duquesne. But, Braddock had unknowingly lured his troops into an awaiting ambush. Indians and French troops, hiding behind trees, opened fire on their unsuspecting foes. The British troops, although much larger in size, were easy targets in their bright red uniforms; and many of them were slaughtered without a fight. The Indians specifically targeted the British and the American officers, knowing that if they were eliminated, the remaining soldiers would scatter in fright. To their delight, every single mounted officer was gunned down.

All … Except for one.

Although he had two different horses shot out from under him, George Washington was the only officer to escape gunfire. After hours of a brutal slaughter when General Braddock was finally shot, Washington assumed control of the troops and led them in a retreat to safety. When Washington returned to their base at Fort Cumberland, he wrote to his mother and his brother to assure them of his safety, giving all due credit to the providence of God:

"By the miraculous care of providence I have been protected beyond all human probability or expectation … For I had four bullets through my coat and two horses shot under me, yet escaped unhurt. Although death was leveling my companions on every side of me."

Word of Washington's miraculous survival spread quickly. Indians and American colonists alike sang his praise. In fact, one Indian chief, who was instrumental in securing the French victory, shot at Washington 11 different times without hitting him! And because this chief's rifle was known as the one that never missed its mark, he finally ceased firing at Washington, convinced that the "Great Spirit" protected him.

But, it wasn't just his dignity as a bulletproof leader that illuminated his character; it was his dignity as a man of God. In 1775, Washington stepped up in a big way to show the world *what* and *whom* his country was going to stand for. In battle or otherwise, each country proudly flew its flag atop its ship—openly and visibly—so that fellow ships could avoid firing at the wrong ships. But, America didn't have a flag. They weren't even a country yet. So, how were they going to recognize their fellow ships? By creating their very first flag, of course. According to official records, this flag had a white background, with a pine tree in the middle, and included the motto, "Appeal to heaven." This was our nation's first flag! And it flew in our navy! It was becoming abundantly apparent—America would be a country that openly and visibly relied on the providence of God.

Only one year later, the Continental Army was ripe with revolutionary spirit, and military tensions were running high. Washington, like many others, had been waiting for this declaration of war for some time, and he had grown impatient with congressional delegates who had hoped to reconcile with Britain.

Even as Washington's men stood before him waiting to hear their leader speak, hundreds of British ships were beginning to occupy New York Harbor, preparing to attack. But Washington—bold and resolute, poised and proud—stood on the steps of city hall overlooking his men and read aloud the Declaration of Independence.

When he was done, the raucous crowd of soldiers, so moved by the words of Washington, raced down Broadway toward a large bronze statue of King George III. They toppled the massive sculpture, cheering as the statue toppled to the ground, crumbling into a cluster of crushed bronze. Soldiers collected fragments of the monument since the bronze could be melted down to be used as bullets—bullets that would be vital in forthcoming battles to defend New York and the young nation that lay beyond it.

AUGUST 27, 1776

Although his army was outnumbered 4:1, short on ammunition, and still suffering the devastating effects of smallpox, Washington was determined to hold New York in the battle of Long Island, but it was not to be.

As quickly as the first official battle of the Revolutionary War began, it ended. Under General William Howe, the British caught American forces by surprise. Nearly 300 of Washington's men were killed. Eight hundred were wounded. More than 1,000 were taken prisoner. Washington was humiliated.

AUGUST 29, 1776

To further his campaign of destruction, General Howe prepared to attack Brooklyn. Washington realized that an open war would assure defeat and the likely end to this great American experiment, but surrender was unthinkable.

Washington began to realize that the only hope of winning the war was not to lose it. Time would become Washington's greatest weapon. But, Washington continued to pray fervently for a stroke of divine providence.

With all of the land routes blocked by British troops, he ordered a retreat across the East River. He immediately sent orders for every feasible seagoing vessel to be collected in the area.

Providentially, nearly a thousand men had arrived only the day before to reinforce Washington's army, including a band of Massachusetts fishermen, who were known to be the best mariners in the Western world. To ensure the British wouldn't discover the American retreat, Washington set out in the dead of night.

Heavy rains, strong winds, and high tides all combined to hinder the British from discovering the retreat, but it also wreaked havoc with Washington's daring plan. The sailboats were of little use in the relentless storm, and only a small number of rowboats was able to be employed.

But, just before midnight, the wind ceased and the water became so eerily calm that the boats could actually be loaded with extra weight. As they embarked, a gentle breeze arose from the south, which carried Washington and his men into New York by the guile of night. However, as the tumultuous weather faded, a new problem was created. Under the light of a full moon, they were certain the British would spot them. Now in plain view of the enemy's encampment, all they could do was pray.

The American retreat continued through the darkness of the pre-dawn sky, and as the sun began to rise, hundreds of troops had yet to be withdrawn. But, out of nowhere, a dense fog began to permeate.

> As the dawn of the next day approached, those of us who remained in the trenches became very anxious for our own safety ... At this time, a very dense fog began to rise and it seemed to settle in a peculiar manner over both encampments ... I recall this providential occurrence perfectly well, and so very dense was the atmosphere that I could scarcely discern a man at six yards distance ... We tarried until the sun had risen, but the fog remained as dense as ever. —Continental Army Officer Benjamin Tallmadge

Suddenly, they were spotted, only it wasn't by British troops, but by a British family who lived near the American encampment. Taking notice of the covert plan, the lady of the house sent one of her servants with a message to warn the British of what was taking place.

When the young servant arrived at the British outpost, the soldiers didn't make much of his story but were sent to validate it nonetheless. Cautiously, they approached the American encampment.

It was empty.

As they panned their eyes toward the East River, the fog had lifted just enough for them to spot four boats in the distance.

They were the last four boats to leave.

The fog had remained until the very last boat left Long Island. Nine thousand men, with nearly all of their horses, guns, provisions, and other supplies, had retreated into New York, untouched.

Too often we look for visible signs, significant gestures, and unthinkable miracles to be the only depictions of God's providence. Sometimes they are, but Washington knew that sometimes God's will could carry a gentle fog just as a mighty thunderstorm.

General Washington and his men were able to safely retreat across the East River that night, but the American war effort was still dire. Washington's soldiers were beginning to lose hope, and the foundation of the young American nation seemed to be weakening. At the first of the year, most of the soldiers' service would be complete, not to mention, defeat after defeat had brought the young nation's morale to its lowest point.

Washington knew he had to make a bold move and go on the offensive, but he couldn't go at it alone. He continued to hold a firm reliance on the protection of divine providence.

> While we are zealously performing the duties of good citizens and soldiers, we certainly ought not to be inattentive to the higher duties of religion. To the distinguished character

> of Patriot, it should be our highest glory to add the more distinguished character of Christian. —George Washington

CHRISTMAS NIGHT, 1776

British General William Howe had long settled down in his luxurious quarters to wait out the harsh winter. General Washington, with the morale of his men waning and the survival of his nation in jeopardy, wasn't quite ready to hibernate.

In a desperate gamble, Washington decided he and his men would cross the Delaware River in the pre-dawn hours and surprise British forces in what would become the Battle of Trenton. Washington knew that the enemy's accustomed drinking on Christmas night would help to assure success for the Americans to slip by unnoticed.

Suddenly, without warning, a massive snowstorm pummeled the area. Fortunately for the Americans, this forceful act of nature worked in their favor, provoking the enemy's watchmen to seek cover and reducing visibility to near zero.

That night, General Washington led some 2,400 men across the ice-filled Delaware River in a blizzard. Trudging through the blinding snow, upon landfall at Trenton, Washington's men took their positions behind trees and attacked the enemy's camp at daybreak.

They attacked so unexpectedly and with such surprise that nearly 1,000 prisoners were taken captive after less than an hour of fighting. German Hessian mercenary troops hired by King

George III were trained to fight in an open field and were not prepared for Americans firing from behind every tree.

> The hurry, fright and confusion of the enemy was not unlike that which will be when the last trump will sound ... Providence seemed to have smiled upon every part of this enterprise. —Henry Knox

Only nine Americans were wounded in the battle. General Howe had missed yet another opportunity to bring the American Revolution to a speedy end.

> Forasmuch as it is the indispensable duty of all men to adore the superintending providence of Almighty God ... And it having pleased Him in His abundant mercy ... To crown our arms with most signal success. —Second Continental Congress

AUGUST 1777

Overconfidence, poor communication, and indecision in the higher ranks soon began to plague British occupation.

General John Burgoyne took command of the northern British armies. He proposed to bisect the American colonies. His men would advance from Canada while another force moved in from upstate New York. Meanwhile, General Howe's men would travel up the Hudson River to bolster these troops, leading to a culminating attack force of over 11,000 men. The strategy was set. The pieces were in place. A deciding day for the revolution had dawned.

However, in haste to leave London for a vacation, British Prime Minister Lord North forgot to sign the official dispatch approving General Howe's war plan. The dispatch was never even sent. Without approval from the prime minister, General Howe and his men would never make the trek, which led to British forces sitting idly by, waiting for an approval that would never come.

As American reinforcements continued to join in the war effort, the British sustained another setback—their reinforcements were left stranded at sea due to harsh weather conditions.

With his hands tied, General Burgoyne pulled back to Saratoga, New York. What he didn't know was American General Horatio Gates and his band of troops were already dug in at Saratoga to greet Burgoyne and his retreating companies.

General Burgoyne was surrounded. Dumbfounded and sensing defeat, Burgoyne—gleaming in his scarlet, gold, and white uniform—surrendered to the plain, blue-coated Gates on October 17, 1777. Most of General Burgoyne's 5,700 soldiers were imprisoned, while General Burgoyne was allowed to flee back to England.

> This glorious revolution ... Distinguished by so many marks of the divine favor and interposition ... In a manner so singular, and I may say miraculous, that when future ages shall read its history, they will be tempted to consider a great part of it as fabulous ... Will it not appear extraordinary ...

> Like the emancipation of the Jews from Egyptian servitude.
> —Chief Justice John Jay

> That with one heart and one voice the good people may express the grateful feeling of their hearts ... Join the penitent confession of their manifold sins ... That it may please God, through the merits of Jesus Christ, mercifully to forgive and blot them out of remembrance, and under the Providence of Almighty God, secure for these Untied States the greatest of all human blessings, independence, and peace.
> —Second Continental Congress

DECEMBER 1777

Even with a victory at Saratoga, the tribulations for American forces were far from over, and the coming winter proved to be the key turning point in the American Revolution.

Upon their arrival at Valley Forge, General Washington's soldiers were frail and indisposed. Nearly one-third of the troops were unfit for duty, and as winter progressed, so did their hardships. Hunger became a great danger. The army frequently went days without food. On days that they did receive provisions, half a cup of rice and a tablespoon of vinegar were the norm.

Hundreds of troops fell sick. During January and February, over 4,000 soldiers were incapacitated due to frostbite, disease, and malnourishment. Many of their feet froze until they became black, and it was often necessary to amputate them.

The men were weary, and their garb was worn. With limited bedding available, the troops longed for a moment's reprieve. They had no clothes to cover their nakedness, no blankets to lie on, and no tents to sleep under. Their countenance was wearing thin.

> Men are confined to hospitals, or in farmers' houses for want of shoes. We have this day no less than two thousand eight hundred and ninety-nine men in camp unfit for duty, because they are barefoot and otherwise naked ... For the want of shoes their marches through frost & snow might be traced by the blood from their feet, and they were almost as often without provisions as with them. —George Washington's letter to Congress. (December 23, 1777)

Yet, in the midst of all this, these men found comfort in the faith and courage of their commander-in-chief, General George Washington.

From the very beginning, Washington tirelessly traveled throughout the camp bringing encouragement to his men, with his very presence giving them strength. His heart was for his men, as well as for his country.

> I feel superabundantly for them, & from my soul I pity those miseries which it is neither in my power to relieve or prevent.
> —George Washington

A young Quaker, who lived near Valley Forge, witnessed Washington's faith up close:

> I tied my horse to a sapling and went quietly into the woods, and to my astonishment, I saw the great George Washington ... On his knees ... Alone. He was at prayer to the God of the armies of heaven, beseeching Him to interpose with His divine aid, and for the cause of the country and of humanity, and for the whole world. Such a prayer I never heard from the lips of man. We never thought a man could be a soldier and a Christian, but if there is one in the world, it is Washington. —Isaac Potts

Also of great comfort: Washington's wife, Martha. It is said she visited the army's encampment every winter throughout the course of the Revolutionary War while fighting was at a standstill. It would take her several days to make the arduous journey from her home in Mt. Vernon, Virginia, to join her husband each winter, but it was very important to her—and to Washington and his troops. Martha would make several rounds a day, visiting soldiers, providing hot meals when they were available, sewing their garments, and nursing the sick. Her commitment to the welfare of the soldiers would remain life-long. In appreciation, soldiers often referred to her as "Lady Washington."

Blood was not shed in battle at Valley Forge, yet these men shed much blood. The blood that stained the ground did not rush forth in the frenzy of war; rather, it fell drop by drop from the heart of a suffering people.

But, Washington knew the cause for which they fought was well worth any price—even the suffering at Valley Forge. Those who endured the bitter cold and snow did not fight for conquest, but they did fight for the freedom to govern themselves. They sought liberty, not only for themselves, but also for the entirety of the world and the generations who were to follow. They fought and they died in the hopes that freedom might be the heritage of all. It was Washington's character that helped sustain the army, but what sustained Washington: Complete faith in God. There was no doubt that Washington was a Christian. He frequently ordered his men to seek the face of God and to observe days of prayer, fasting, and thanksgiving. American General Henry Knox was one among many who gave testimony of Washington frequently visiting secluded groves to lay the cause of his bleeding country—in prayer—at the throne of grace.

Over 200 years later, President Ronald Reagan would remark on Washington's unyielding faith in his National Day of Prayer Proclamation:

"The most sublime picture in American history is of George Washington on his knees in the snow at Valley Forge. That image personifies a people who know that it is not enough to depend on our own courage and goodness; we must also seek help from God, our Father and Preserver."

JANUARY 1778

While Washington's men endured the harsh winter at Valley Forge, news of the American triumph at Saratoga reached Paris, France, where it was celebrated almost as if it were a French victory. The year prior, France had taken their first step toward aiding America, sending 14 ships with crucial military supplies to the new nation. In fact, most of the Continental Army's gunpowder in the first few years of the Revolutionary War came from France.

The American victory at Saratoga led to the signing of two crucial treaties in 1778: The Treaty of Amity & Commerce and the Treaty of Alliance. Under these treaties, France not only acknowledged the United States as a nation, but they also agreed to fight alongside their newfound allies until American independence was won. For the United States, this meant more troops, and much needed financial aid would begin to pour in. The Continental Congress acknowledged this as the hand of God and declared a National Day of Thanksgiving.

> It having pleased the Almighty Ruler of the Universe propitiously to defend the cause of the United American States, and finally by raising up a powerful friend among the Princes of the earth, to establish our Liberty and Independence upon a lasting foundation; it becomes us to set apart a day for gratefully acknowledging the Divine Goodness, and celebrating the event, which we owe to His benign interposition. —George Washington

MARCH 1778

In Valley Forge, a bitter winter was finally coming to an end. With the approach of spring and the health of soldiers improving came another welcome sight to General Washington and his soldiers: the arrival of Friedrich Wilhelm von Steuben.

A veteran Prussian soldier, Steuben arrived in Valley Forge to offer his services to the Continental Army. No one could have been more valuable at the time. Even as Washington had given the troops confidence as men, Steuben's rigorous drilling and training gave them confidence as soldiers.

He was firm with the troops—instructing them on the fundamentals of close-order drill, how to march in formation, and how to properly handle their weapons. They were finally molding into a well-disciplined army. Not only had godly character been instilled within the army by Washington, but at last, military skill had been imparted to them by Steuben.

By the end of 1778, the British succumbed to defeat in the northern colonies, so they redirected their focus on a new strategy—a southern invasion, starting with key ports along the Atlantic Seaboard. The whole region from Virginia southward had been mostly free of battle during the war, and King George III desperately sought a victory to improve the morale of his men.

Over the next two years, British forces stunned the southern colonies. The redcoats quickly occupied the thriving town of Savannah, Georgia, as a spearhead for their new strategy. They continued northeast toward Charleston, South Carolina, and then onward to Camden, occupying both cities, and pillaging homes along the way.

American forces moved north, ahead of the pursuing Brits, in hopes of luring General Cornwallis and his band of redcoats to Virginia, where American reinforcements were already waiting, setting the stage for a final showdown.

But, even though the Americans retreated in haste, the Brits were quickly gaining ground. Often, Cornwallis would catch up to them, but time and time again, a providential turn of events would stall their effort. It seemed every time the redcoats tried to cross a river, some colossal storm would appear out of nowhere, flooding the waters before them and halting their pursuit. Three times this happened—from the Catawba River, to the Yadkin, and onward to the Dan.

Even British Commander Henry Clinton acknowledged that divine providence intervened in favor of the Americans:

> Here, the royal army was again stopped by a sudden rise of the waters, which had only just fallen, to let the enemy over, who could not else have eluded Cornwallis' grasp, so close was he upon their rear. —General Henry Clinton

Meanwhile, General Washington's troops, primed and ready for battle, began their trek southward to prepare for the siege in Virginia.

All roads led to Yorktown.

OCTOBER 5, 1781

Washington's troops arrived on the outskirts of Yorktown and began to dig their first parallel. American reinforcements from the south arrived soon after. The heavily overcast sky negated a full moon above and shielded the massive digging operation from the eyes of British outlooks. Washington struck the first several blows into the ground with his pickaxe to begin the trench. The trench was 2,000 yards long, running from the head of Yorktown to the York River. Over the next several days, troops completed gun placements and dragged the artillery into line, awaiting their foe.

By October 9, British troops had spotted the trench, just out of musket range. What they witnessed stunned them. They weren't expecting that amount of firepower. Without reinforcements, British General Cornwallis was barely holding out against the American siege. He was outnumbered 2:1. In a panic, he decided to attempt a retreat across the York River just before nightfall.

The roles had been reversed. Cornwallis was now using Washington's tactics.

> ... But at this critical moment, the weather, from being calm, changed to a violent storm of wind and rain, and drove all the boats down the river. —General Cornwallis

Unable to complete his intended retreat due to the inclement weather, Cornwallis found his already mismatched force divided. The Americans had them surrounded. Cornwallis, sensing defeat, surrendered his forces to General Washington, marking the end to the final battle of the Revolutionary War.

Eight thousand British soldiers reversed their muskets, lowered their flags, and ceremoniously marched in sorrow as drummers and fifers played, "The World Turned Upside Down."

> Resolved, that Congress will, at two o'clock this day ... Return thanks to Almighty God, for crowning the allied arms of the United States and France, with success, by the surrender of the Earl of Cornwallis. —Second Continental Congress

> The General congratulates the army upon the glorious event of yesterday. Divine service is to be performed tomorrow in the several brigades and divisions. The commander-in-chief recommends that the troops not on duty should universally attend with that seriousness of deportment and gratitude of heart, which the recognition of such reiterated and astonishing interpositions of Providence demand of us. —George Washington

Whatever lingering hopes of victory the British may have harbored vanished at the Battle of Yorktown.

"Oh God, it's all over," British Prime Minister Lord North groaned at the news of Cornwallis' surrender.

On February 27, 1782, the British House of Commons voted against continuing on with the war. Three weeks later, Lord North resigned, but it wasn't until September 3, 1783, under the Treaty of Paris, that Great Britain finally recognized the independence of the United States of America. The Revolutionary War was officially over.

George Washington went on to become the first president of the United States of America. On April 30, 1789, he took the oath of office with his right hand placed on the Word of God. At the end of the oath, he added the words, "So help me God," leaned over, and kissed the Bible, starting a tradition that every president since has followed.

> It would be peculiarly improper to omit, in this first official act, my fervent supplications to that Almighty Being who rules over the universe, who presides in the councils of nations ... No people can be bound to acknowledge and adore the Invisible Hand which conducts the affairs of men more than the people of the United States. Every step by which they have advanced to the character of an independent nation seems to have been distinguished by some token of providential agency ... We ought to be no less persuaded that the propitious smiles of Heaven can never be expected on a nation that disregards the eternal rules of order and right which Heaven itself has ordained.
> —from George Washington's Inaugural Address

Few foreign observers thought that the upstart American revolutionaries could win a war against the world's greatest empire. It was like David versus Goliath. But, the patriots proved their critics wrong, forcing the British redcoats to their knees.

The British dispatched two-thirds of its entire army and one-half of its formidable navy to suppress the American revolt—a stunning statistic that reflected not only the tenacity of the patriots but, also, the difficulties facing the British Empire as they tried to conduct a far-flung campaign thousands of miles from home. Their costly military endeavors maintained elsewhere around the globe, and the intervention of the French on behalf of the Americans was the straw that broke the camel's back, forcing their hand at granting independence to the Americans.

But, the most crucial facet of all was America's unbending faith in divine providence. Throughout the war with Great Britain, the Second Continental Congress and men like George Washington frequently declared days of fasting and prayer to beseech God for guidance and success in their struggle for freedom. It was faith that established America's independence and providence that secured the most free and prosperous nation the world has ever seen.

Suppose you had been a delegate to the Second Continental Congress when the debate for independence had ended and the voting began. How would you have voted? Sure, it is easy for us to say 'yes, of course,' but too quick an answer may reveal that we haven't really thought about the situation our Founding Fathers were facing. Great Britain was the most powerful nation on earth at the time. Defeating them seemed hopeless. It was militarily impossible. We were out-gunned, out-manned, out-supplied, and out-generaled. From a human point of view, waging this war was the height of foolishness. It was a national death wish.

But, our Founding Fathers were hardly fools. They cast themselves on the mercy of God. And although the vast majority of them were Christians, even the few unbelievers among them voted for independence and understood the impact that faith had on the lives of their fellow citizens.

The Founding Fathers felt that the struggle for their God-given, unalienable rights of life, liberty, and the pursuit of happiness were so important that they were willing to sacrifice themselves fighting for it. They had come to the position of Esther in the Old Testament when she risked her own life to petition the king: *"If I perish, I perish."*

Our Founding Fathers relied on the Word of God, and to this day, that Word is still the one true voice of freedom that resounds throughout the world.

James Madison writes an essay for The Federalist Papers.

CHAPTER 6

CHRIST IS THE END OF THE LAW

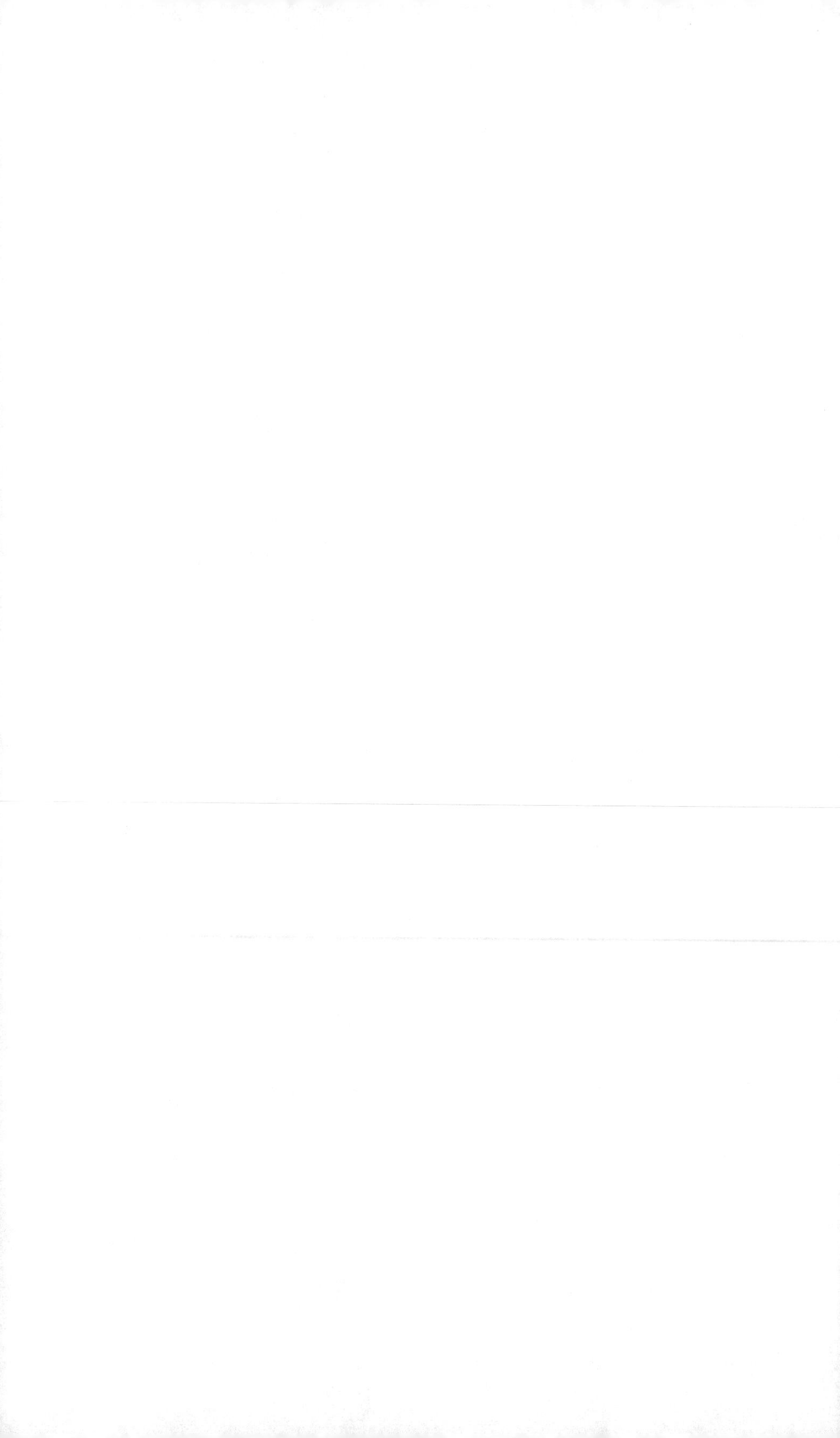

CHAPTER SIX

CHRIST IS THE END OF THE LAW

The United States of America shocked the world as it defied and conquered the most powerful empire in the world, thus bringing an end to the Revolutionary War. Now the newly crowned citizens of America faced a new and unprecedented challenge: a nation founded in faith needed to craft a capable and functioning government—a framework that would not only champion the principles of freedom and liberty but, also, uphold the standard of biblical conviction.

Throughout the course of history, there is a distinct relationship between a people who choose the gospel and their achievement of freedom. As long as the Word of God is a nation's foundation, freedom and liberty will be its inheritance. After the British signed the Treaty of Paris, ending the Revolutionary War, freedom and liberty were inherited by the new American nation, but the fight to sustain that freedom and liberty had only begun.

During the war, the American people's resentment of British imperial rule led them to create the Articles of Confederation, a governing document that decentralized power and granted sovereignty to the states. As Thomas Jefferson declared, "Virginia, sir, is my country." Such powerful local ties help explain why Americans focused their attention on creating state constitutions rather than one powerful national government.

But, the Articles of Confederation provided only the semblance of national authority. It kept the states together in wartime, but there remained an unrelenting pressure to create a permanent and lasting government—a new government that learned from the flaws of the previous regime and gave the power back to "We the people."

> If men were angels, no government would be necessary. If angels were to govern men, neither external nor internal controls on government would be necessary. In framing a government which is to be administered by men over men, the great difficulty lies in this: you must first enable the government to control the governed; and in the next place oblige it to control itself. —James Madison, Federalist No. 51, February 6, 1788.

MAY 14, 1787: PHILADELPHIA, PA.
INDEPENDENCE HALL

Only 13 years earlier, America's Founding Fathers sat in the same room and put their "lives, fortunes and sacred honor" on the line before a lengthy war with the world's most formidable military. The Pennsylvania State House had been renamed Independence Hall for that heroic act, yet a different spirit was among the delegates in the room on this day—angst and uncertainty.

The Constitutional Convention was plagued with problems before it even began. Only seven of the 13 states showed up—some of those only by a partial delegation. And there was no funding. The delegates who came did so at their own expense.

The conglomeration of delegates quickly shifted into two distinct groups: the Federalists and the anti-Federalists.

The anti-Federalist leaders—Patrick Henry, George Mason, and Richard Henry Lee—were men whose careers and reputations had been established well before the Revolution. Their names held weight among the people, and they were respected among their peers.

In contrast, the Federalist leaders—Alexander Hamilton, John Jay, and James Madison—were much younger men whose careers had just begun amid the Revolution. They were recognized by the people but didn't have the same level of favor or sway like the Anti-federalists.

From the first call to order, the struggle between these two groups was ferocious.

The anti-Federalists were cautious and claimed the carnal nature of man. They wanted power to remain in each state's jurisdiction and fought against a dominant national union.

The Federalists, on the other hand, emphasized the importance of Christian character and virtue given by the providence of God during the Revolution. They yearned for a strong national government that could carry weight in representing the American cause to global powers.

The eruption of dissension between the Federalists and the anti-Federalists was merciless. The delegation was quickly spiraling into a vicious contest. Neither side would budge, and everyone had an opinion. When they were drafting the Declaration of Independence, more than half of the delegates held divinity degrees; this time, more than half of the delegates were lawyers.

George Washington mediated as leader of the Constitutional Convention, but he had very little success.

> If, to please the people, we offer what we ourselves disapprove, how can we afterward defend our work? ... Let us raise a standard to which the wise and honest can repair; the event is in the hands of God —George Washington

Eighty-one-year-old Benjamin Franklin, the oldest delegate, said very little from the floor but provided a wealth of experience and common sense behind the scenes.

> It is a common observation here that our cause is the cause of all mankind, and that we are fighting for their liberty in defending our own —Benjamin Franklin

Although there were veterans with distinct name recognition (like Washington and Franklin) attending the Constitutional Convention, it was another man (a young man) who quickly emerged as the central figure of the event, making a name for himself and eventually earning the title, "Father of the Constitution." That man was James Madison.

Small of stature, and frail in health, the 36-year-old bachelor was shy and socially awkward. Crowds made him nervous, and he avoided using his high-pitched voice in public, much less in an open debate. But, the Princeton graduate possessed an agile mind and had a voracious appetite for learning. His baggage was invariably stuffed with various books and scores of notes. He had been preparing for the convention for years and knew more about historic forms of government than any other delegate on the floor. But, the well-prepared Madison found a worthy opponent in political veteran, Roger Sherman.

For every ounce of intelligence that Madison had, Sherman responded in kind with wisdom only time and experience could provide. Throughout the convention, Sherman called for more than 160 different motions. Not to be outdone, Madison called for more than 175. Among them, Madison proposed a revolutionary idea: that the delegates scrap their intentions to revise the Articles of Confederation and submit an entirely new document to the states.

He proposed three separate branches of government—legislative, executive, and judicial—aiming to form a federal government that made laws for all citizens. Being a delegate from Virginia, Madison dubbed it "The Virginia Plan."

Seeing that pamphlets and essays were the best form of swaying public sentiment, the anti-Federalists started publishing essays under the pen name "Brutus," pertaining to the Roman who assassinated Julius Caesar to prevent him from overthrowing the Roman government and seizing control as emperor.

James Madison and company responded in kind, distributing the more optimistic and well-written "Federalist Papers." Known simply as "The Federalist," this provocative collection of essays was originally published in New York newspapers between 1787 and 1788. In the end, 85 essays were published under the pen name "Publius," meaning the common man. Alexander Hamilton wrote 50; Madison authored 30 more, and the remaining 5 by New Yorker, John Jay. Written in support of ratification, the essays defended the principle of national authority but sought to reassure doubters that the people and the states had little reason to fear a return to tyranny in the new government.

In perhaps the most famous "Federalist" essay (Number 10), Madison argued that the very size and diversity of the expanding nation would make it nearly impossible for any single faction to form a majority that could dominate the government.

> Extend the sphere, and you take in a greater variety of parties and interests; you make it less probable that a majority of the whole will have a common motive to invade the rights of other citizens. —James Madison

The conventional wisdom of the time was that republics could only survive in small, homogenous countries like Switzerland and the Netherlands. Large republics, most thought, would fragment, dissolving into anarchy and tyranny through the influence of factions. But, Madison insisted, given a balanced federal government, a republic could work in large, diverse nations even better than in smaller nations. Madison and the other Federalists also insisted that the new union would promote prosperity by reducing taxes, paying off the national debt from the war, and expanding the economic influence.

The anti-Federalists, however, weren't giving in. Dictators possessed evil impulses and sinful natures, they argued, abusing their power to enhance themselves and oppress the masses—a power they had become all too familiar with under British rule. Not only did Patrick Henry, one of the most outspoken anti-Federalists, refuse to attend the Constitutional Convention, but he also demanded that it be investigated as conspiracy and treason. Animosity had reached a boiling point over the law of the land. Benjamin Franklin had restrained himself from most of the proceedings but could not stay quiet any longer.

> The small progress we have made after 4 or 5 weeks is melancholy proof of the imperfection of the Human Understanding. We need the Father of lights to illuminate our understandings! During the war, our prayers, Sir, were heard, and they were graciously answered. And have we forgotten that powerful friend—Great Britain? Or do we imagine that we no longer need his assistance? I have lived, Sir, a long time, and the longer I live, the more convincing proofs I see of this truth—that God governs in the affairs of men. And if a sparrow cannot fall to the ground without his notice, is it probable that an empire can rise without his aid? We have been assured, Sir, in the sacred writings, that 'except the Lord build the House

> they labor in vain that build it.' I firmly believe this; and I also believe that without his concurring aid we shall succeed in this political building, no better than the builders of Babel ... We shall be divided by our little partial local interests; our projects will be confounded and we ourselves shall become a reproach and bye word down to future ages ... I therefore beg leave to move that, henceforth, prayers imploring the assistance of Heaven and its blessing on our deliberation be held in this assembly every morning ... And that one or more of the clergy of this city be requested to officiate in that service. —Benjamin Franklin (addressing the Convention)

Benjamin Franklin's call for prayer marked the turning point of the Constitutional Convention. Yet, who would know it? Modern historians and professors tell a different story—a story that all but disallows the evidence of God's providence.

As Americans, we must re-discover the basic truths of our nation's history. Christianity is engrained within the smallest microfibers of America's fabric. It is wrought into America's social, civil, and political institutions.

Historian Jedidiah Morse agreed. Having studied theology at Yale University under Jonathan Edwards, Morse went on to become not only a preacher of the gospel but, also, one of America's first historians.

> The office of historian is to record the progress of human affairs as directed by the Providence of God; to exhibit the connection of events, showing how an immense series is

> produced as cause and effect, and lastly to display the character of man and God. —Jedidiah Morse

How many historians today would speak so freely about the connection between the affairs of men being guided by the providence of God? Sure, there are a few here and there, but they are a distinct minority drowned out by those who would rather disconnect faith from all historical accounts.

Our society today is much like that of the ancient Israelites, who lost the Word of God in the dusty corners of the temple archives. The Bible plainly warns us of this in Proverbs 29:18 when it says, *"Where there is no vision, the people perish."*

Modern history paints a picture of the Founding Fathers as nothing more than deists or universalists. However, for the majority of these men, their Christian faith was, indeed, at the forefront of their lives. Our Founding Fathers' own words confirm that they rejected any notion that America was anything less than a Christian nation.

> The originators and early promoters of the discovery and settlement of this continent, had the propagation of Christianity before their eyes, as one of the principal objects of their undertaking ... Christianity was intended by them to be the cornerstone of the social and political structures which they were founding. —James Madison

> The general principles on which the fathers achieved independence were the general principles of Christianity. I will

> avow that I then believed, and now believe, that those general principles of Christianity are as eternal and immutable as the existence and attributes of God; and that those principles of liberty are as unalterable as human nature. —John Adams

> Here is my creed. I believe in one God, the Creator of the universe. That He governs it by His providence. That He ought to be worshipped. —Benjamin Franklin

By the same token, one should not deify the Founding Fathers. They weren't perfect. Many biblical scholars aren't even sure that Benjamin Franklin was a true, born-again Christian.

However, one must remain true to history. If the founders were largely men of faith, then it is inconceivable that they would establish policies to limit expressions of that faith. If these men were by and large a collective group of atheists and agnostics, then it would stand to reason that the founders would want nothing to do with the like when constructing a national governing document.

When the framers of the Constitution found themselves in their darkest hour, just moments away from dissolving the union they had fought so hard to create, they turned to prayer. Benjamin Franklin called for divine intervention—not once, not twice, but every single day. And it's important to note, Franklin's call to prayer wasn't addressed to some vague or ambiguous God; it was to the one true God, the Creator of the universe, the God of Christianity.

According to intellectual elitists, Franklin was a marked deist. But, one of the tenets of deism is that God doesn't interfere with the affairs of men. Well, why then would Franklin say that the older he gets, the more he realizes that God governs in the affairs of men? Maybe Franklin was a Christian; maybe he wasn't. But, when the chips were down, he knew what his country needed. As soon as the delegates began to call upon the Lord, the convention began to see progress. The factions began to work together to see what they could agree on instead of focusing on what they did not. Suddenly, the spirit of competition became a spirit of collaboration.

The Committee of Detail was appointed to write the first draft of the United States Constitution. Five men were chosen for the committee: Edmund Randolph, Oliver Ellsworth, John Rutledge, James Wilson, and Roger Sherman. All five of these men were Christian.

Borrowing political ideas from Montesquieu, a French philosopher during the Age of Enlightenment, the American government would consist of three separate but equal branches. The executive office would enforce the law and conduct foreign policy. The judicial branch would hear court cases, provide sentencing, and interpret the constitution concerning justice. The legislative branch would write and amend all laws proposed.

The committee agreed to these basic tenets of government, but while proposing the legislative branch, discord again reared its head. The northern states wanted equal representation in the branch while the southern states wanted representation proportionate to each state's population. The northern states took issue with that since the southern states had higher populations if slaves were included in the count. Whoever won this battle would have clear control over the legislative branch. A compromise had to be made.

James Wilson and Roger Sherman proposed the 3/5s compromise. It stated that each slave was to be counted toward representation as 3/5s of a whole. Essentially, for every 5 slaves, 3 votes would count. This compromise not only appeased both sides, but it also kept the factions on equal footing concerning control of the legislature.

The foundation for the Constitution of the United States of America was set and ratification soon followed. Several of the smaller states were among the first to act:

Order of Ratification:

1. Delaware – December 7, 1787
2. Pennsylvania – December 12, 1787
3. New Jersey – December 18, 1787
4. Georgia – January 2, 1788
5. Connecticut – January 9, 1788
6. Massachusetts – February 6, 1788
7. Maryland – April 28, 1788
8. South Carolina – May 23, 1788
9. New Hampshire – June 21, 1788

10. Virginia – June 25, 1788

11. New York – July 26, 1788

12. North Carolina – November 21, 1789

13. Rhode Island – May 29, 1790

The representation of clergymen in this process proved to be crucial.

In Connecticut, Reverend William Samuel Johnson testified to his state's convention that the harmonious system of government coming out of Philadelphia was "a sign of God's almighty hand."

In Massachusetts, as many as 20 clergymen served as delegates in their state convention, and the vote to ratify the new U.S. Constitution came down to 19 votes: 187 for, 168 against. One of the men even urged ratification on the grounds that this union was "the rock of their national salvation."

In South Carolina, celebration broke out when the ratification vote was announced to the state delegates. When order was restored, an elderly statesmen, Christopher Gadsden, declared, "I shall say with good old Simeon, *'Lord, now lettest Thou Thy servant depart in peace, for mine eyes have seen the salvation of my country.'*"

Upon notification that New Hampshire had become the ninth state to ratify the Constitution, Congress began to draft plans for the transfer of power to the new federal government created by the Constitution.

Some remained cautious ...

> Our constitution is in actual operation. Everything appears to promise that it will last; but in this world nothing is certain but death and taxes. —Benjamin Franklin

Others relied on their faith ...

> Should everything proceed as we anticipate, it will be so much beyond anything we had a right to imagine or expect 18 months ago that it will demonstrate the finger of Providence in human affairs greater than any event in history. —George Washington

And providence reigned in America ...

> The religion which has introduced civil liberty is the religion of Christ and his apostles, which enjoins humility, piety, and benevolence; which acknowledges in every person a brother, or a sister, and a citizen with equal rights. This is genuine Christianity, and to this we owe our free constitutions of government. —Noah Webster

I'm sure many of you are thinking it, how can the Constitution be considered a Christian document when it doesn't specifically refer to God or to the Word of God? Well, there was a valid reason for that. The delegates came from 13 different states, and most had their own state churches. There was a general agreement that the federal government would not establish any of those state churches as the new federal church.

A religious reference would have only created divisions. And the last thing this young American nation needed was division within its own ranks. It required everyone to come together for a common cause—for the sake of preservation.

> The Constitution was made only for a moral and religious people. It is wholly inadequate for the government of any other. —John Adams

However, a reference to religion would come shortly thereafter within the first 10 amendments to the Constitution, known better as the Bill of Rights. If America were to have a strong national government, the people would need to have their own set of liberties and rights immune to federal usurpation. The Bill of Rights allowed the citizens to be given the authority to be the system of checks and balances for the federal government.

The combination of the First and Second Amendments alone provides a unique component to the Constitution that had never before been implemented in other societies: freedom. That component provided protection for citizens against the government, freedom of speech, and the right to bear arms. But, most importantly, it ensured the freedom of religion, and with it, the prevention of religious oppressions experienced in England and other societies prior to 1776.

> It had become an universal and almost uncontroverted position in the several states that the purposes of society

> do not require a surrender of all our rights to our ordinary governors ... And which experience has nevertheless proved they (the government) will be constantly encroaching on if submitted to them; that there are also certain fences which experience has proved peculiarly efficacious (effective) against wrong and rarely obstructive of right, which yet the governing powers have ever shown a disposition to weaken and remove. Of the first kind, for instance, is freedom of religion. —Thomas Jefferson

The First Amendment states: "Congress shall make no law respecting an establishment of religion, or prohibiting the free exercise thereof; or abridging the freedom of speech, or of the press; or the right of the people peaceably to assemble, and to petition the government for a redress of grievances."

It has since been referred to as the "separation of church and state," but what did the First Amendment really mean when it was written? The question of church and state is an issue that continues to perplex our country. Battles are continually waged over this issue—in schools, courts, and on the campaign trails. Many people, including Christians, are confused about their relationship to one another. Some have fallen prey to the propaganda that, by its lack of an official establishment clause, the Constitution states there should be no relationship between God or Christianity and the government. No assertion could be further from the truth. Upon the conclusion of the Constitutional Convention, George Washington stated, "One could trace the finger of Providence through those dark and mysterious events." That doesn't sound like the statement of a man who intended to separate God and government.

In 1820, Thomas Jefferson completed a comprehensive version of the Bible, incorporating more than 50 moral teachings from the four gospels of the New Testament. He called it *The Life and Morals of Jesus of Nazareth.* Most people know it today simply as the "Jefferson Bible."

Jefferson arranged these teachings in chronological order and translated them into English, French, Latin, and Greek. He described these teachings as the "most sublime and benevolent code of morals, which has ever been offered to man." According to Jefferson, lessons from Jesus served as reasonable guidelines for the life of every citizen. Since there were so many other leaders who echoed that same sentiment, congressmen were actually given a copy of the Jefferson Bible whenever they were sworn into office.

In a Christian nation, the people make the laws, but the church makes the people. When the church fails to necessitate a moral influence, the spirit of the Constitution and its purpose in law and order will not work.

Our Founding Fathers, while not all born-again Christians, firmly believed in the biblical ideas of man and government. They believed that man's sinful nature meant that he should not be entrusted with too much power, even if he was reborn through the blood of Jesus Christ. The form of government you determine depends greatly on whether or not you believe mankind has an inherent sin nature. In the Federalist Paper No. 51, James

Madison stated, "What is government itself but the greatest of all reflections on human nature?"

When the delegates gathered in Philadelphia for the Constitutional Convention in the spring of 1787, most of them were expecting to amend the existing Articles of Confederation. But, some of the delegates were prepared to draw up an entirely new document altogether—a document that would formulate a system of government powerful enough to prevent anarchy but appropriately restricted to prevent tyranny.

The drafting of a new U.S. Constitution provoked strong opinions and heated debates regarding national power, states' rights, and the basic freedoms of all citizens. The delegates all had good intentions, but there were nearly as many opinions as there were delegates. Their basic worldview was the same, but it seemed everyone had their own approach. There was anger; there were disputes. But, the power for preserving this great republic was placed directly into the hands of the people, and for the most part, the delegates' differences on political philosophy fell within a narrow range—disagreeing more over means than ends. Few of the Constitution's supporters liked it in its entirety, but most believed that it was the best document obtainable. And they all desired the same thing: a free and Christian nation ... With liberty and justice for all.

The delegates didn't intend to put new and untried ideas into practice. These men were intelligent, well educated, and widely read. They based their political concepts on facts and combined the best ideas they read about to establish a successful government. But, without a doubt, the greatest embodiment of this document is its Christian influence. In the Preamble, it is stated that civil government exists to "secure the blessings of liberty." Leviticus 25:10 states: *"Proclaim liberty throughout all the land unto all the inhabitants thereof."* Blessings are a gift from our Creator, not a privilege granted by government. The Constitution shaped the Founding Fathers' core vision for America: that God sets men free, it's their natural right to have liberty, and each is made to rule with Christ.

The durability and flexibility of this document testifies to the remarkable men who made it. The delegates were surprisingly young. At an average age of 42, they were farmers, merchants, lawyers, and bankers. Many of them were widely read in history, law, and political philosophy. Ordinary men, yet they were practical men of experience, tested in the fires of the Revolution. In fact, 21 of the delegates had served in the conflict. Seven had been state governors, most had been members of the Continental Congress, and eight of them had signed the Declaration of Independence.

The Constitution of the United States of America has provided a solid model of government whose features have been repeatedly borrowed by other nations through the years. Yet, what makes the U.S. Constitution so distinctive is not its many compromises or specific provisions, but its remarkable harmony with the people it governs. The Constitutional Convention didn't just create "a more perfect Union" in 1787; it engineered a frame of government whose resilience has enabled later generations to experience, first-hand, what the Founding Fathers set out to do.

In 1789, Americans wildly celebrated the inauguration of George Washington as the nation's first president. But, amid the excitement was a powerful undercurrent of uncertainty, suspicion, and anxiety. The Constitution provided a living framework of government ... Not a blueprint. Many questions were left unanswered, and unexpected challenges lay on the horizon. But, the heartbeat of providence was still beating in America.

> We have staked the whole future of American civilization, not upon the power of government, far from it. We have staked the future of all of our political institutions upon the capacity of mankind for self-government; upon the capacity of each and all of us to govern ourselves; to control ourselves, to sustain ourselves according to the Ten Commandments of God. —James Madison

Charles Finney preaches at a revival in New York City.

CHAPTER 7

AS FOR ME AND MY HOUSE

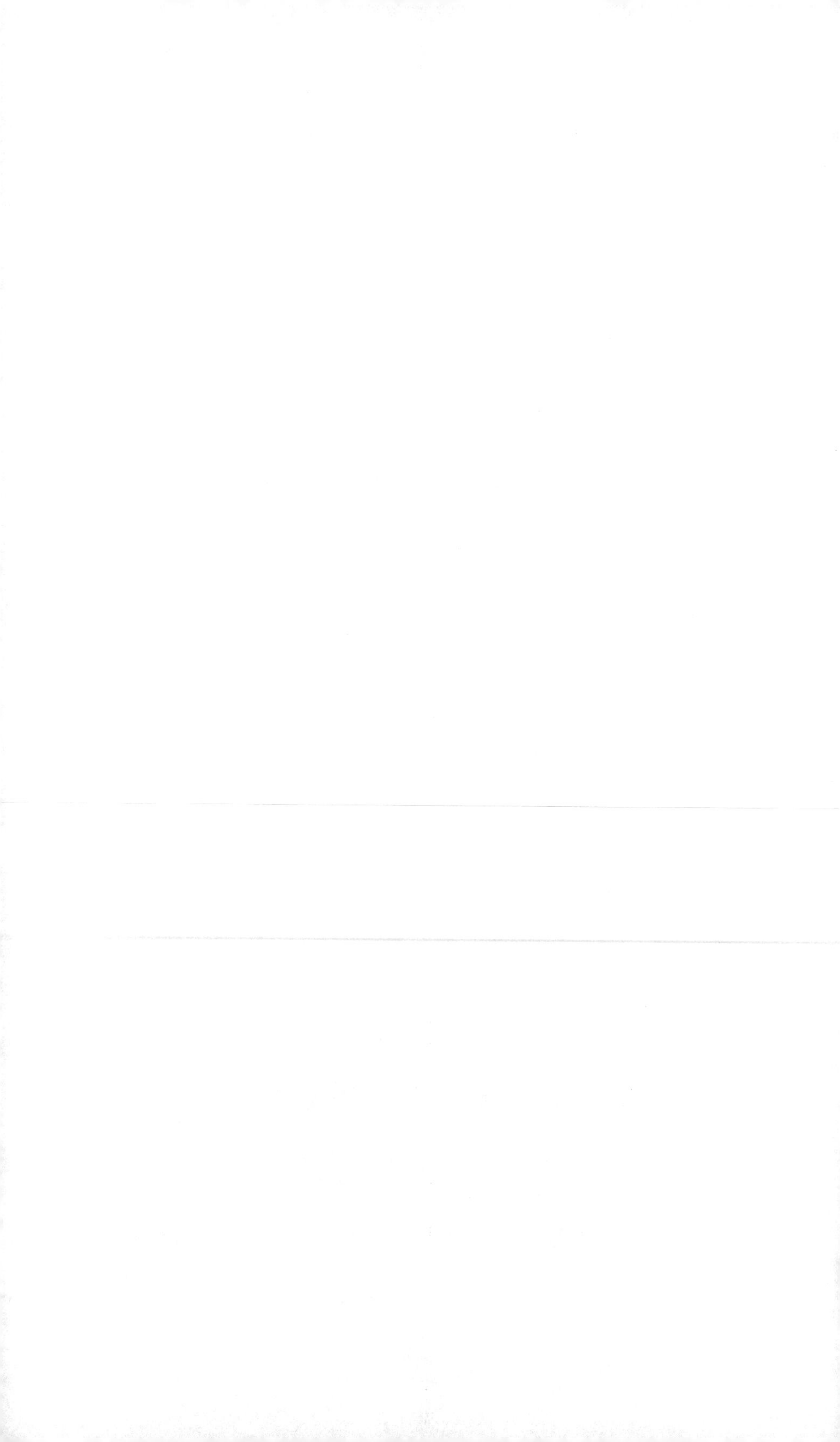

CHAPTER SEVEN

AS FOR ME AND MY HOUSE

With America's Constitution now in place, its new government was up and running, but how would the nation develop? What would be its destiny?

The Constitution of the United States was constructed on the firmly laid foundation of the Declaration of Independence. The Preamble of the Constitution concisely adopted the principles of the Declaration and adapted those principles to build a structured form of government—a representative republic. This young republic would represent the moral fortitude of its founders and the spiritual values of its people. It would be evident that this new form of government was built on the bedrock of biblical principles.

"The American national consciousness," one observer wrote, "is not a voice crying out of the depth of the dark past, but is proudly a product of the enlightened present, setting its face resolutely toward the future."

American exceptionalism was the embodiment of a stirring ideal. Since the arrival of the Pilgrims, many thought of America as a chosen vessel for a special role in God's great plan, as the Constitution put it, to ensure the "the blessing of liberty."

Pastor Jonathan Edwards said God chose America as the "glorious renovator of the world." John Adams proclaimed America as a "grand scheme and design in providence for the illumination and the emancipation of the slavish part of mankind all over the earth." This mission Adams spoke of was the call to lead the world toward greater liberty, but there were problems that still needed to be addressed.

Before the Revolutionary War, colonists knew only struggles—the struggle to survive, the struggle to overcome oppression, the struggle to break away from the bonds of tyranny. But, having accomplished the unimaginable in victory over the British, citizens now found themselves in their own country, living in peace. With men like Thomas Jefferson, George Washington, and John Adams laying the foundation for the growing nation to stand upon, how could anything go wrong?

Nothing born of God can remain untested, and a great trial was on the horizon for the young American nation. At the dawn of the 19TH century, people's activities began to drift in different directions, drawing distinct divisions in three regions of the young country. In the north, it was industry; in the south, agriculture; and in the west, expansion. However, just like the years before the first Great Awakening, an over-privileged populous began turning their backs on God once again. America's worldly pursuits were taking priority, and they were leaving providence in the dust.

> The American war is over: but this is far from being the case with the American Revolution. On the contrary, but the first act of the great drama is closed. —Benjamin Rush, 1787

The United States of America was beginning to prosper in the new century. Many who lived and fought in the Revolutionary War were finally able to use their gifts and talents for a greater purpose. Samuel Slater built the nation's first modern textile factory. Oliver Evans developed the first fully mechanized flour mill. Eli Whitney invented the cotton gin.

Transportation was developing rapidly. In 1794, the first all-weather toll road was built in Pennsylvania. Layer after layer of crushed stone was packed down and finished with a mixture of rock dust and water. When the mix dried, it was like cement, giving America its first paved roads. For the horses and oxen accustomed to pulling heavy wagons across the country down dirt roads and muddy passageways, it was a welcome improvement.

Transporting goods swiftly and across long distances still remained a great challenge, but American innovation led to the idea of digging the Erie Canal. New York Governor DeWitt Clinton conceived the idea, and with it blossomed a nation-changing innovation. Canals were now being built up and down the Ohio and Mississippi River systems, providing an efficient and economical new way of shipping.

One of God's greatest gifts to the United States is its system of rivers, but at the turn of the 19TH century, America had barely begun to tap into its potential. Rafts and barges had long been used to ship cargo downstream, but traveling upstream was another story. That is, until 1807 when a New Yorker by the name of Robert Fulton demonstrated American ingenuity with the invention of a steam-powered boat. Two-way commerce was now a reality, and the efficient use of the river systems was fully realized.

As the infrastructure for shipping goods expanded, so did the ability to spread the Word of God. Evangelists and missionaries embarked into the American frontier, bringing with them only their Bibles and the conviction to carry Christianity onward into the ever-expanding Western horizon.

In the years following the War for Independence and the signing of the Constitution, America transitioned from war and strife to freedom and liberty. For many, moving past the violence of war and political turmoil was a difficult task, but for others, it was finally time to reap the benefits for which they had fought so long.

Thomas Jefferson found himself working ceaselessly, moving from one public office to another, but always moving upward, both in prominence and power. He served as governor of Virginia, diplomat to France, secretary of state, vice-president, and, eventually, the president of the United States.

As president, Jefferson understood the benefit to Native Americans having the access to the Word of God. Knowing the power of the gospel, he wanted to provide it to the indigenous population, but he was given council that the King James Bible would only confuse the Native Americans. In response, President Jefferson personally condensed and consolidated the biblical teachings of Jesus Christ into what he aptly named *The Philosophy of Jesus of Nazareth* in 1804. This companion text allowed the native nations to read about Jesus in a simpler form.

Modern historians often skew the facts when referencing this work. They claim that Jefferson was isolating the moral philosophy of Jesus and did not include miraculous events. But, the healing of the sick, the casting out of demons, the raising of the dead, and the resurrection of Jesus are all included in *The Philosophy of Jesus of Nazareth.* His work was wildly successful, so he continued to work on it for several more years.

By 1820, Jefferson had completed the task and renamed his work, *The Life and Morals of Jesus of Nazareth.* Nearly 60 years later, one U.S. senator who read the publication was so stirred by it that he compelled the United States government to print it and provide a copy to every congressman and senator for the next 50 years.

Benjamin Franklin was also able to transition back into civilian life after his retirement from politics. Two of his most important works were the invention of bifocals and the discovery of electricity. Most of us know the story—Franklin standing outside with a key attached to his kite in the middle of a thunderstorm. This discovery quickly led people to understand the powers that electricity could hold for humanity. Many of the words associated with electricity were actually coined by Franklin—words like battery, charge, and conductor—but even more importantly, this led to the invention of the lightning rod.

Throughout history, humankind had seen lightning as physical proof of the divine. Thor threw bolts from the sky in Nordic mythology, Set held the reins of the sky in Egyptian mythology, and Zeus cast lightning from Mount Olympus in Greek and Roman mythology. The old wives would say that if lightning struck your home, it was ordained by God. Even some Christians thought that lightning was exclusively divine intervention. Matthew 24:27 says: *"For as the lightning cometh out of the east, and shineth even unto the west; so shall also the coming of the Son of Man be."* In Habakkuk 3:11, it says, *"The sun and moon stood still in their habitation: at the light of Thine arrows they went, and at the shining of Thy glittering spear."* For many Christians, lightning was the medium of the Almighty and should not be tampered with, but Franklin wrote to his skeptics, "It has pleased God in his goodness to mankind, at length to discover to them the means of securing their habitations and other buildings from mischief by thunder and lightning." With that statement, he shook the foundations of religion and traditions. Benjamin Franklin said that science was not in opposition to faith in God, but that science was a gift from God and evidence of His goodness to mankind.

A lesser-known but equally important founding father, Benjamin Rush, was essential to the American Revolution, both in the war campaign and in establishing a new society. Educated at Princeton University, Rush was a prominent advocate for many causes, including the abolition of slavery, treatment for the mentally ill, and women's rights. He spent time in Europe and was fluent in French, Italian, Spanish, and also studied Latin for his medical career. It was Rush who trained and advised Lewis and Clark prior to their journey westward. It was Rush who lobbied for educational standards and prison reform. It was Rush who reconciled John Adams and Thomas Jefferson in their later years. But above all other endeavors, his faith was held highest.

> I do not believe that the Constitution was the offspring of inspiration, but I am as perfectly satisfied that the Union of the United States in its form and adoption is as much the work of a Divine Providence as any of the miracles recorded in the Old and New Testament. —Dr. Benjamin Rush

Unlike the nations of the Old World, which had storied histories, the United States was an infant republic swaddled in the Age of Enlightenment.

A period of innovation and idealism had enveloped the young American landscape, but as the country flourished, the church and faith in Christ became secondary, exactly like those colonists prior to the first Great Awakening. Just as the dream of liberty was coming to fruition, America was slipping into a state of spiritual and moral decay.

In times of great hardship and war, many flocked to the church to cling to the Lord's comfort. Now, with newfound freedom and prosperity, they grew prideful in their own abilities and felt these many achievements were solely their own.

With innovation came expansion, and the people of America were spreading westward. When the Pilgrims set foot on the shores of America in 1620, they envisioned close-knit communities built on Bible teachings. That dream, now realized, was taken for granted as more and more Americans became too busy for the church, too busy to read the Bible, too busy for God. The young American nation was asleep, intoxicated by the ill-informed illusion of their own personal greatness. They were now in desperate need of another spiritual wake-up call.

Throughout the course of history, it is easy to see people's spiritual commitment rise and fall with ebbs and flow of life. During tumultuous times, dusty church pews will quickly be filled with those seeking comfort, those seeking refuge, and those seeking God.

But, moving forward as a newly unified republic, the people of America trusted time to heal their hearts instead of the Lord. God was put on the back burner once again.

When we are pushed to the limits and our backs are against the wall, Christians depend on their faith in the Lord. Why? Because in times of trouble, He is the only one that can carry us when we fall, or mend us when we are broken, or light the path when we've lost our way. But, an equally difficult test is how we react when God blesses us. How do we respond to prosperity?

It might remind one of the children of Israel. After arriving in the Promised Land, the manna that sustained them for 40 years was no longer provided. It ceased because they had entered into the Promised Land. After years of depending on God in a wild frontier to provide them with manna, they finally had to work for their provisions, and they survived.

For early Americans, survival was their new reality. The struggle for freedom and liberty had been brutal. They relied on God while their necks were pinned under the jack-booted heel of King George, but could their faith survive during the time of plenty?

New generations unfamiliar with that brutal struggle of the past had grown complacent. They were prideful because they didn't pay a personal cost for their freedom as the founding generation had. Historian Peter Marshall called this time the "Great Asleepening." With the foreign and external threats gone, people were forgetting that darkness and sin could also lie within.

The first Great Awakening was a lightning strike, which sparked a spiritual flame in the hearts of patriots and preachers who led the revolution. What America needed now was a lightning *storm*—a storm to set the entire nation aflame. As the first Great Awakening had been God's revival for America's leaders, the second Great Awakening was a revival for its people.

In the year 1800, the spiritual climate of the new American century was growing cold. People held on to their church affiliations very loosely, if at all.

In the north, the once booming attendance at Presbyterian and Congregational churches waned. In the south, the once well-established Anglican church had weakened, suffering the stigma of being aligned with the Church of England. In order to diminish their pro-British image, many Anglicans renamed themselves "Episcopalians" following the revolution, but the change in name couldn't prevent the denomination from losing its luster in the south.

From town to town and state to state, once vibrant churches now resembled museums—old buildings, antiquated furnishings, lifeless souls.

But, the potential for revival was still there, if desired. Christianity in America was in critical condition. There was barely a pulse. Vital signs were low. The heart of the church needed to be electrified—zapped back to life. It needed a shock to its system to survive.

At last, the lightning struck.

THE CANE RIDGE REVIVAL

Vanderbilt historian, Paul Conkin, called it "arguably ... The most important religious gathering in all of American history."

While it wasn't the first event of its type, its scope and scale were turning more than a few heads. People from all over Kentucky had come to see what God was doing. He was awakening souls by the thousands.

Organized by the Reverend Barton Stone, this great Camp-meeting greeted more than 20,000 people—⅛ of the state's entire free population. The crowds overwhelmed Stone, who had only planned for 2,000, but he had invited seasoned frontier preachers from all denominational backgrounds to the revival. Stone invited these men in hopes that they would serve as one heartbeat—a spiritual heartbeat of revival. And each preacher brought his own congregation to hear the anointed gospel of Jesus Christ. As the preachers preached, the Holy Spirit fell upon the crowd. Congregants wailed under heavy conviction of their sins, seeking salvation. Ministers would stay through the night, preaching and leading people to Christ.

There was singing; there was shouting—an uncommon sight in that day.

The power of God was moving.

> The campground was well illuminated; the people were differently exercised all over the ground, some exhorting, some shouting, some praying, and some crying for mercy, while others lay as dead men on the ground. —John McGee, a Methodist preacher

But, with such a great and visible manifestation of the Holy Spirit came excess. Some fell into a trance; some got down on all fours and began barking like dogs.

And not everyone was onboard. Older mainline denominations scoffed, professing it purely emotionalism.

Peter Marshall wrote, "There were many instances of hard cases and scoffers falling at the continual services 'as suddenly as if struck by lightning,' sometimes at the very moment they were cursing the proceedings."

Many came to the revival as skeptics but left as believers. One such skeptic described the scenes in front of him with such vivid detail that one can truly envision what was occurring.

"The noise was like the roar of Niagara. The vast sea of human beings seemed to be agitated as if by a storm. I counted seven ministers, all preaching at one time, some on stumps, others in wagons. Some of the people were singing, others praying, some crying for mercy in the most piteous accents, while others were shouting most vociferously."

The Sunday morning service was the tipping point of the Cane Ridge revival. As congregants gathered to take the Lord's Supper, a mighty move of the Holy Spirit swept over the crowd. Thousands began crying out to the Lord. Souls were saved. As the Reverend Barton Stone told it, "A particular description of this meeting would fill a large volume, and then the half would not be told."

What took place at this Campmeeting shook the very foundation of the frontier—a monumental moment not only in American history but, also, in church history.

The second Great Awakening was alive.

Following Cane Ridge, revival quickly spread all throughout Kentucky, Tennessee, and southern Ohio, leading to an efficient organization known as "circuit riding." Promoted primarily by Methodist and Baptist ministers, these circuit riders were the evangelists of their day. They traveled from town to town, seeking out people in remote locations, striving to establish a lasting rapport with frontier families.

Like the Campmeeting, circuit riders kept the fires of revival burning in remote frontier towns. Ministers found ready and willing audiences among the lonely western landscape. They were hungry for the Holy Spirit and yearning for a spiritual community.

The successes of these circuit riders were pivotal to the second Great Awakening. By the 1840s, the numbers of Methodists and Baptists rivaled that of the Anglicans, Presbyterians, and Congregationalists—denominations that had dominated during the colonial period.

African Americans were especially attracted to the new Methodist and Baptist churches. Richard Allen, who would later help to found the African Methodist Episcopal Church, said in 1787:

"There was no religious sect or denomination that would suit the capacity of the colored people as well as the Methodist."

Allen realized that this plain and simple approach to spreading the gospel suited all people, no matter their social status or level of education. According to Allen, the Methodists were the first denomination to "bring glad tidings to the colored people."

The Baptist church followed suit. Like the Methodists, they offered a gospel of salvation open to all, regardless of wealth, social standing, gender, or race.

Freemen and slaves alike worshipped in these congregations, infusing their different cultures into one community of worship.

These revivals offered a redemptive social outlet to isolated rural communities, primarily the women, for whom the Camp-meetings provided an alternative to the rigors and loneliness of farm life. Evangelical ministers now applauded the spiritual fortitude of women and affirmed their right to give witness to their faith in public.

Some of these women became traveling evangelists themselves. Phoebe Palmer, for example, hosted prayer meetings in her own home in New York City for several years before taking to the road, traveling all over the United States. These opportunities to assume what had been traditionally male roles bolstered women's self-worth and expanded their horizons beyond the domestic sphere—a monumental achievement in women's rights.

Before the events of the Cane Ridge revival, not many had ever heard of a Campmeeting, and its meaning was simple: a revival lasting several days, with people traveling from near and far to take part in a shared time of Christian fellowship, praise, and worship—a time of devotion, a time of healing, a time of blessing.

Early in the 19TH century, a Campmeeting was simply that—a *camp* out. There were no modern conveniences on the frontier. Families would travel for days from towns far and wide to hear the preaching of circuit riders and evangelists. They constructed camps. Tents of canvas and cloth were fashioned in open fields. Local vendors would set up shop through the week, selling goods to the visiting families.

These Campmeetings would build dozens of raised wooden platforms, spread over hundreds of yards across the encampment, so that multiple preachers could minister at the same time without their voices impeding one another.

Spiritual lightning was striking all over the country.

Francis Asbury quickly became one of America's greatest spiritual Founding Fathers. No, he didn't sign the Declaration of Independence, he didn't help frame the Constitution, and he never served as president of the United States or in any other political office of government. He was, however, one of God's chosen vessels, carrying the gospel of Jesus Christ through a new and developing American nation.

Asbury established a mobile brand of evangelism that was perfectly suited to the frontier environment. He scoured the Appalachian frontier for lost souls, covering more than a quarter of a million miles by horseback! He personally ordained more than 4,000 preachers and preached more than 16,000 sermons over the course of his ministry.

His message changed thousands of lives during his lifetime, weaving together the spiritual fabric of the American frontier. He labored to bring the greatest form of freedom to a land that had become far too complacent with its newfound liberty.

The second Great Awakening was spreading like wildfire throughout the United States. In the north, older denominations were awakened once more. Slavery and alcoholism waned as preachers convicted their crowds with sermons of abolition and temperance. Education and women's rights were emboldened as the Bible was heralded as the center of understanding and wisdom.

However, in the southern states, the Methodists and Baptists were seeing a different story unfold. The social reform movements of the north did not have the same effect where slavery was so deeply engrained in the culture and economy. Approaching that polarizing issue with caution, ministers would appeal to the hearts and minds of the individuals, preaching the gospel to change each person from the inside in the hopes that God would light their way. The ministers trusted the Holy Spirit to do the work.

The second Great Awakening for the northern and southern states was a revival of the Spirit like the rekindling of embers in a dying fire. Though many were Christian in name only, at least there was a foundation for the preachers to build on.

Prior to the second Great Awakening, most pioneers saw circuit preachers as a form of entertainment. It was something to take their minds off of the long days and the harsh lives of homesteaders. In frontier life, if you had a problem, you had to deal with it yourself. You had little support to protect you from Indian attacks, unrelenting weather, disease, and starvation, but as the wildfire of revival raged through the Appalachian Mountains, frontier families realized that Christian fellowship would be the answer.

Preachers made their way westward, though not as gentle orators, but Spirit-filled drill sergeants. Drunkenness, violence, and sexual promiscuity were attacked. The covetous, the thieves, the swindlers, and the fools were all directly brought to charge. Psalms 23:4 says, *"Thy rod and Thy staff they comfort me,"* but the Lord uses that staff not only in protection but correcting the direction of his flock. These Methodist and Baptist circuit riders didn't come as lambs to pander philosophy, but as lions to roar the Word of God, and when God's preachers don't hold back, neither does God. Bars closed and churches opened. Families were restored as husbands joined their wives and children at home instead of escaping to the inside of a bottle.

Entire communities were transformed as the drunken shanties and raucous revelry switched to songs of praise and worship and cries of admonition. Like rotting and overripe fruit, America's spiritual self had fallen away into a state of decay, but during the second Great Awakening, a new seed sprouted in the heart of America. America as a nation had been born again.

As believers, we often lose our way. We're only human after all. We start off our Christian walk with the Lord with vigor and fire, but in one fell swoop, the world, the flesh, and the Devil can grab us right by the throat and choke the ever-living breath out of us. History shows us, however, that the providence of God is always at work. During times of great apathy, He is not asleep.

As revival spread across the country, another reformation was taking place among the young people. The *New England Primer* had been used for nearly a hundred years as the most basic textbook for schools in the colonies. Based upon the English title, *The Protestant Tutor,* the *New England Primer* had served many Americans well during its time.

It was meant to be a consolidated teaching resource for basic reading and writing—a tool for students to memorize idioms easily so they could recite them while working in the fields or learning their trade.

Starting with the letter *A,* students were to learn that, "In Adam's fall, we sinned all." For the letter *B,* "Thy life to mend, this Book attend," speaking of the Bible. Many of its references were biblical and based on the King James Bible.

Primary schools in early 19TH century America were often overcrowded. Sometimes up to 70 students were crowded into a schoolhouse with no desks, outdated textbooks, and led by a single teacher. Levels of learning were not separate; therefore, the students' progress was often slow and frustrating, but God called one man to change that.

Noah Webster studied at Yale during the American Revolution under Ezra Stiles. It was here that he connected the Bible and its infallible connection to learning.

> The education of youth, an employment of more consequence than making laws and preaching the gospel, because it lays the foundation on which both law and gospel rest for success. —Noah Webster

Noah Webster looked at the deplorable situation in American schoolhouses and surmised solutions to solve the scholastic issues in America. He wrote and released a three-volume compendium named, *A Grammatical Institute of the English Language.*

Among his many suggested changes, he rejected the requisite learning of Greek and Latin before learning English. He also proposed that learning should be broken into smaller classifications that could eventually build up to more advanced notions. So, he set forth a system of levels, which pupils must master before moving on to the next. For example, young children should first learn the English alphabet, studying vowels and consonants, before moving onto learning how the letters make up words. From learning words and their meanings, they could then use the words to form simple sentences and then compound sentences. This may be commonplace in the modern world, but when Noah Webster proposed these ideas, they were seen as revolutionary.

The system was an instant success, but Webster found another problem. Concerning the words being taught, a wide variety of textbooks was being used, and most were grossly outdated—hundreds of years old in some cases. Webster wanted to create a high-quality resource for the benefit of all students. In 1806, he began writing what we now know as *Webster's Dictionary.*

> Education is useless without the Bible. The Bible was America's basic textbook in all fields. God's Word, contained in the Bible, has furnished all necessary rules to direct our conduct. —Noah Webster

It took Webster over 25 years to complete his dictionary. During that time, he learned and studied over 27 languages to provide authenticity to each definition—its etymology and its root language. But definitions were not the only thing included in the original publication of *Webster's Dictionary*. Each word was also used in a sentence, and what do you think Webster used? That's right—Bible verses. Webster considered education useless without the Word of God.

> In some countries the common people are not permitted to read the Bible at all. In ours, it is as common as a newspaper and in schools is read with nearly the same degree of respect. —Noah Webster

He used his dictionary to emphasize faith in the Word and constantly referred to the fear of God as the basis of all understanding. He would go on to write *The Value of the Bible and Excellence of the Christian Religion*—a book written to join his years as an educator to his growing involvement with politics. He would write:

> Every civil government is based upon some religion or philosophy of life. Education in a nation will propagate

> the religion of that nation. In America, the foundational religion was Christianity. And it was sown in the hearts of Americans through the home and private and public schools for centuries. Our liberty, growth, and prosperity was the result of a Biblical philosophy of life. Our continued freedom and success is dependent on our educating the youth of America in the principles of Christianity.
> —Noah Webster

During the second Great Awakening, Christian education was no longer for a select few; it was now freely available to all people in America. Through *Webster's Dictionary* and his new system of learning, generations of Americans would now depend on the Bible as the cornerstone of their education.

As education reformation began to take shape in America's children through Webster's efforts, God would begin to call forth other men to reach the young adults in higher education.

Enter Timothy Dwight, the president of Yale College. He resolved to purify a campus that had turned into a "hotbed of infidelity." For more than seven years, Dwight, grandson of the great revivalist Jonathan Edwards, preached a series of weekly sermons on the doctrines of Christianity ... on a college campus ... at Yale! Oh, did I mention Yale originated as a Christian college?

The students were captivated. In his first year of teaching and ministry alone, nearly half of the student body gave their hearts to the Lord. One man wrote, "Yale College is a little temple; prayer and praise seem to be the delight of the greater part of the students while those who are still unfeeling are awed with respectful silence."

The fervor of revival fanned the flames of righteous renewal across the country and was compared to that of a fast-moving forest fire. Just like evergreen forests, a cleansing fire is necessary for new growth as the ashes of the excess provide nourishment for new life. Western New York, in fact, experienced such intense levels of evangelical activity that it was labeled the "Burned Over District." The most successful evangelist in the Burned Over District was quite literally the spiritual successor of Timothy Dwight. His name was Charles Finney.

Finney was a vibrant, fiery lawyer, but under Dwight's ministry at Yale, he quickly felt the call of God in his life. He would bring that same righteous fire to the pulpit. Finney preached marathon "fire and brimstone" revivals, often lasting for hours at a time. He carried the methods of the frontier revival to the cities and factories of the east and as far as Great Britain.

In 1835, Finney accepted the professorship of theology at the newly established Oberlin College. From the start, Oberlin College radiated the spirit of reform, predicated on faith. Oberlin was the first college in America to admit women and black people. It would be a grassroots hub of the anti-slavery abolition movement.

Finney's dynamic personality paved the way for his success as an innovator of evangelism. He brought about many changes to the American church—changes that were practically unheard of before his time. He organized choirs for praise and worship, and actively advertised and promoted his revivals so that people could plan months in advance to attend. Many also consider him to have shaped the modern concept of the altar call, but perhaps one of the greatest hallmarks of his ministry was reform.

As a strong proponent of the abolition of slavery, Finney believed the gospel did not merely effect the salvation of a soul but could also cure the ills of society. He encouraged Christians to get involved in their communities, and he worked tirelessly to see society changed by the gospel of Jesus Christ.

> Where there is no religion, there is no morality ... With the loss of religion ... The ultimate foundation of confidence is blown up; and the security of life, liberty, and property are buried in ruins. —Timothy Dwight

The fires of revival carried over oceans just as easily as it carried over mountains. Europe was washed in revival as circuit riding and Campmeetings took place in the land of kings and queens, which had only 50 years prior held the leash of America. Still, the spiritual fires swept over the world as missionaries moved on to Africa, Asia, and South America. The spreading of the gospel gave the 19TH century an appropriate nickname: the Protestant century.

The Holy Spirit cleansed the Protestant church through revivals, but outside the walls of worship, many began to believe that social reform was also a part of God's plan. Local churches started to see their roles in society as more than just an isolated institution. They intended to purify their communities through their spiritual influence.

Temperance, abolition, and women's rights became the targets of reform in the early 19TH century. Activists of these social movements encouraged the preservation of family and community through the abstention of alcohol, the abolition of slavery, and the birth of women's rights.

While religion had previously played an important role on the American political scene, the second Great Awakening highlighted that role and demonstrated how individuals' beliefs would play a part in the new American century.

Individuals like Lyman Beecher, one of the towering champions of revivalism, stressed that the second Great Awakening was not focused simply on promoting individual conversions to Christ, but it was also intended to reform human society. He took a harsh stand against the abuse of alcohol from behind the pulpit and went on to publish several of his sermons—sermons that quickly found their way into the hands of thousands of Americans and eventually across the Atlantic, being translated into multiple languages on the European continent.

Lyman Beecher passed his legacy for reform on to his children. His son, Henry Ward Beecher, was one of the most respected evangelists of his day and became a staunch advocate for women's rights. His daughter, Harriet Beecher Stowe, took on the role as a devoted abolitionist and went on to publish one of the most cherished novels in American history, *Uncle Tom's Cabin*. Harriet Beecher Stowe was a shining example of how the second Great Awakening was able to facilitate changes for so many people. After all, it would have been thought impossible only 50 years before—a female author writing a story that promoted Christian values, the equality of women, and the abolition of slavery. Not only was that story published and widely read, but even more importantly, it fundamentally altered the lens through which the nation viewed these issues. The winds of change were blowing, and the Lord was leading the way.

David Livingstone was another iconic figure during the second Great Awakening. With a strict Calvinist upbringing, David Livingstone knew the importance of living for God and spreading the gospel to all corners of the world.

At the age of 19, Livingstone began medical training at Anderson's College in Glasgow, Scotland, but he remained fascinated with theology. Initially, when he joined the London Missionary Society, he wanted to begin his missionary work in China. But, under the persuasive tactics of Robert Moffat, one of the most successful missionaries at the time, Livingstone set his sights instead on South Africa.

In 1841, Livingstone took his first expedition to Africa where he covered the expansive Kalahari Desert, preaching the good news of Jesus Christ to the people for more than 11 years. Livingstone's vision was to shed light in a dark place and make Africa well known to people around the world.

Upon his return to Britain, he cut ties with the London Missionary Society to compose a book about his travels with the help of John Murray. *Missionary Travels and Researches in South Africa* became instantly popular, selling out even before the first two publications. Livingstone commented about his written work, "I think I would rather cross the African continent again than undertake to write about it. I intended on going to Africa to continue my studies; but as I could not brook the idea of simply entering into other men's labors made ready to my hands, I entailed on myself, in addition to teaching, manual labor in building and other handicraft work, which made me generally as much exhausted and unfit for study in the evenings as ever I had been when a cotton-spinner. The want of time for self-improvement was the only source of regret that I experienced during my African career."

The difficulty of writing couldn't compare to Livingstone's next journey. The Zambezi expedition proved itself to be arduous. Navigation was difficult and the water too low for passage as a result of the steamboat's poor design. Ultimately, he failed to complete his mission, and many members of his team died from illness, including his wife, Mary. Under the heavy burden of heartache, Livingstone made sail across the Indian Ocean to Bombay for a brief period and then decided to travel back to Britain to recuperate.

The Cross-Continental expedition of 1866 was next on his list. Unfortunately, this exploration also had its fair share of difficulties. He nearly lost all of his trade goods in the harsh journey to Loanda; however, his efforts paid off as he became the first European to travel the entirety of Africa, which sparked his fame.

Livingstone's final journey took place over a seven-year period in which he traveled throughout east and central Africa with a specific focus on the Nile River in order to understand more about the African water systems. Unfortunately, a combination of malaria and dysentery quickly took its toll on

Livingstone, and he died at the age of 60. His final journey became his body's final resting place, but his soul, without a doubt, abides with the Lord.

> I place no value on anything I have or may possess, except in relation to the kingdom of Christ. If anything will advance the interests of the kingdom, it shall be given away or kept, only as by giving or keeping it I shall promote the glory of Him to whom I owe all my hopes in time and eternity.
> —David Livingstone

Another influential American during this time was Harry Hosier. Unfortunately, many people today have never heard about his great efforts to spread the gospel of Jesus Christ.

Harry Hosier, or "Black Harry" as he was more commonly known, was born in North Carolina as a slave, but most historians agree that he obtained his freedom shortly after the conclusion of the American Revolution.

Because Hosier was illiterate, several versions of his name were recorded throughout the years, including Hosier, Hossier, and Hoosier, to name a few. That's why you may see his name spelled different ways in different publications. Ironically, many believe the Indiana "Hoosier" nickname was derived from Harry Hosier.

Although Hosier was unable to read and write, he possessed an undeniable oratory skill that Francis Asbury molded and made known to the public. Asbury recognized Hosier's unique ability to memorize entire passages of the Bible as if he were reading directly from the page. Even so, Asbury wasn't the only one who noticed Harry Hosier's talent.

Benjamin Rush thought it necessary to "make allowances for his illiteracy as he was the greatest orator in America." One example of that skill was evident in a sermon entitled "The Barren Fig Tree." Taken from Luke 13: 6–9, "The Barren Fig Tree" is recorded as the first Methodist sermon delivered by an African-American. Through the success of his preaching, Hosier was able to accompany many preachers, like Asbury, across America by horseback. In fact, Hosier's outreach was so extensive Asbury commented that Hosier drew even larger crowds than Asbury himself.

Although he drew large crowds and became well-known across the United States, Hosier attracted more than his fair share of dissenters. After all, he was a black, illiterate preacher who ministered to both black and white audiences. That was unheard of in those days.

But, despite the ridicule, Harry Hosier went on to preach to audiences far and wide until his death in 1806. After he passed, Hosier's impact on the church only flourished as the United States witnessed a substantial growth in black Methodist preachers. Although most today are unfamiliar with his good works, through it all, Hosier served as an inspiration for thousands of people—breaking racial barriers and championing the gospel of Jesus Christ to his fellow Americans.

As He so often does, God raised up men of the faith to proclaim His gospel at the turn of the 19TH century. Every generation must have its own move of God; it must have fresh manna, or else, it will lose its way. Men like Timothy Dwight, Charles Finney, Francis Asbury, Noah Webster, and Barton Stone were raised for such a time as this. They were a new generation of voices, built on the foundation of bold, anointed preaching of the gospel, crying out to its people, *"Repent: for the kingdom of heaven is at hand."* They were a new generation that desired America as a "city on a hill."

Out of this revival birthed a great spiritual resurgence, fundamentally altering the character of the American landscape. Its people were beckoned back to the Lord.

> There is no country in the history of the world, which Christianity holds a greater influence over the souls of its citizens than America. —Alexis de Tocqueville

The second Great Awakening stirred the waters of America's soul, and God provided the anchor.

Andrew Jackson prepares for the Battle of New Orleans.

CHAPTER 8

THE BATTLE IS THE LORD'S

CHAPTER EIGHT

THE BATTLE IS THE LORD'S

At the dawn of the 19TH century, the United States of America faced a number of challenges. The newly-founded nation was learning how to govern itself as a republic and manage its growth, all the while defining and protecting its borders. America would have to face these new challenges without its fearless leader and first president, George Washington.

Washington chose to step down after two terms as president despite massive popularity and nearly unanimous support. He was held in such high regard that the two terms he served would act as an unofficial term limit for the American presidency, as no president would run in a third general election until Franklin Delano Roosevelt during World War II.

The country was in solid hands, however, as fellow founder and Washington's vice-president, John Adams, took the reins as America's second president. The author of the Declaration of

Independence, Thomas Jefferson, came next, followed by the "Father of the Constitution," James Madison. But, with Madison's presidency came America's next great test.

The defeat of England at the Battle of Yorktown marked the end of the Revolutionary War and the beginning of a new era for the United States of America, but not even three decades after the signing of a peace treaty, the two countries were once again in conflict.

In the eyes of England, America was a house of cards—one that would inevitably fall. To them, it was just a loosely collected group of local governments without a significant military, so what chance did it stand? England began to flex its muscles.

With the Napoleonic Wars raging in Europe, England was running low on sailors and troops, so when the opportunity arose to seize seasoned sailors from American ships that might be supplying goods to France, they jumped at the chance to kill two birds with one stone. This led to the systematic kidnapping of American sailors. Over 6,000 were forced onto British ships. They based the kidnapping of American sailors, a practice known as "impressment," on the notion that they were still subjects of the Crown and were held accountable to British maritime law.

To make matters worse, Great Britain enacted the Orders in Council—trade laws that restricted American commerce with the rest of Europe. American ships would have to dock in British ports, submit to searches, and pay taxes before being allowed to sail onward to the European mainland. England was unilaterally deciding what the United States could and could not do in terms of trade.

In response, the United States enacted a controversial trade embargo at the height of the Napoleonic Wars, making any and all exports from the U.S. illegal. The goal was to force England and France to respect American rights during the war. But, the plan backfired. It led to an economic disaster, wreaking massive unemployment.

By the time Jefferson turned over the presidency to James Madison in 1809, the conflict was reaching a boiling point. From the outset, Madison's presidency was entangled in these foreign affairs and crippled by poor economic policy. Madison and his advisors repeatedly overestimated the young republic's diplomatic leverage and military strength. The results were humiliating and lent credence to the notion that the United States was not to be respected as a world power. Even worse, the American people began to lose faith in the fledgling republic.

With the American economy in shambles, growing resentment among the population, and the impressment of American sailors, the situation looked dire for President Madison and the young nation. Madison made a last-ditch effort to negotiate, finally using the threat of force. But England continued the impressment and ignored Madison's demands.

> The rights of persons, and the rights of property, are the objects, for the protection of which government was instituted. —James Madison

On June 1, 1812, President Madison asked Congress to declare war on Great Britain.

The War of 1812 is known as "the forgotten war," but make no mistake, the soul of the United States was at stake. The young nation hoped to establish itself as a power not to be trifled with, expecting to prove to the world that America was not just some grand experiment, but a stalwart republic built on the bedrock of Christian principles.

When the War of 1812 began, the American army and volunteer militias numbered 6,700. Poorly-trained, ill-equipped, and spread out over a newly expanded border (due to the Louisiana Purchase), U.S. forces were led by aging officers that were well past their prime. The navy was in slightly better shape. American ships were fast and powerful. Able officers and salty sailors were ready for battle. But, there were only 16 ships in the fleet. They were facing the British Royal Navy with a fleet of more than 1,000 ships. Even with Great Britain's focus occupied on the war with Napoleon, the odds were entirely against an American victory by land or by sea. Despite all of these concerns, Madison charged ahead, thrusting an unprepared nation into a war that it had little to no chance of winning.

James Madison quickly realized that he had no George Washington to lead his army or anyone with the savvy diplomatic brilliance of Ben Franklin. Both John Adams and Thomas Jefferson had recently retired to private life, so it was up to James Madison to inspire a new generation of American patriots. Madison, himself, didn't fit the mold of a great leader.

He was studious, soft-spoken, and lacked the soldierly qualities needed to inspire national confidence or lead with great resolve. But, like David turning to God before facing Goliath …

"Then said David to the Philistine, Thou comest to me with a sword, and with a spear, and with a shield: but I come to thee in the name of the Lord of Hosts, the God of the armies of Israel, Whom thou hast defied" (I Sam. 17:45).

… President Madison called for nationwide prayer.

> I do therefore recommend ... Rendering the Sovereign of the universe ... Public homage ... Acknowledging the transgressions which might justly provoke His divine displeasure ... Seeking His merciful forgiveness ... And with a reverence for the unerring precept of our holy religion, to do to others as they would require that others should do to them. —James Madison

Madison implored Americans to trust in providence and turn to God as their defender, but just because God is in your corner doesn't mean you don't have to step up and fight.

America advanced, answering the starting bell. Across the ring was a familiar and powerful foe, the world heavyweight champion, Great Britain, and the first round was underway.

For the first few years of the war, the fighting took place along the Canadian border, and neither country was able to gain an upper hand. But, in 1814, the Napoleonic Wars ended in favor of the British Crown, allowing Great Britain to focus its full military might on the United States of America.

AUGUST 24, 1814

Great Britain moved its naval fleet from Europe to the East Coast of the United States, bringing with them their most seasoned fighting forces, fresh from victory over Napoleon. British troops were landing in droves on the American coastline. They raided Chesapeake Bay and marched largely unopposed into the Capitol: Washington, D.C. British forces marched in formation through the streets of Washington with little resistance. Panic-stricken Americans fled from their homes. The Capitol was captured.

President Madison had been spirited away to safety in rural Maryland, along with the primary founding documents and some of George Washington's letters. The popular First Lady, Dolly Madison, remained behind to host a dinner with the staff, but she received word to abandon the White House just as the food was being served. She and the staff gathered all the valuables they could carry and escaped with only moments to spare. Legend has it that, as they were leaving, Dolly ordered the portrait of George Washington to be taken with them, but the frame was too large to carry, so she ordered the canvas to be cut out in order to preserve the symbol of the great leader. The British were so close behind them that when troops reached the White House, the candles at the dinner were still burning, and the feast was still warm.

British Admiral George Cockburn and his band of redcoats ransacked the White House. They relished in the banquet of

Virginia ham and apple pie left behind. The admiral and a few of his soldiers even sat down at the table and held a mock congress. When he asked who was in favor of burning the Capitol, in unison they all yelled, "Aye!"

The vengeful British set the White House ablaze, igniting an inferno that engulfed the entire block, burning the Capitol, the treasury, Library of Congress, and the navy yard. In fact, they set fire to nearly every public building in Washington. Only the patent office remained untouched.

As the fires lit up the Capitol, storm clouds began to roll in, and the sky darkened. The roaring flames of burning buildings were drowned out by the crescendo of torrential rain. Wind whistled and thunder rolled as a late summer storm enveloped the area. And it moved with incredible speed, seeming to come out of nowhere.

"Great God, Madam! Is this the kind of storm to which you are accustomed in this infernal country?" Admiral Cockburn asked a local woman in the street. She replied, "No, sir, this is a special interposition of providence to drive our enemies from our city."

A dark, spinning funnel of wind began to take shape in the pitch-black sky, and a sound like that of a freight train surpassed even the noises of the already deafening storm. A tornado touched down and screamed down Constitution Avenue, sending debris flying, blowing off rooftops, and knocking down brick walls onto the scurrying British troops. Two cannons were lifted off the ground and dropped hundreds of yards away. Horses and their riders were thrown into the sky and slammed to the ground.

British forces retreated back to their ships only to find several blown ashore and others with damaged riggings. As quickly as it came, the tornado disappeared and a heavy rain fell for several hours more, extinguishing the flames.

> The enemy by a sudden incursion has succeeded in invading the Capitol of the nation. During their possession though, for a single day only, they want only destroyed the public edifices - an occasion, which appeals so forcibly to the patriotic devotion of the American people, none will forget. Independence is now to be maintained with the strength and resources which heaven has blessed. —James Madison

More British soldiers were killed by this providential act of God than from all the firearms American troops had mustered in the feeble defense of their fair city. The violent turn of events dampened both the raging fires and the enthusiasm of British forces. But, even with this divine intervention, America's future seemed uncertain. Washington was destroyed, and the British pressed onward, setting their sights on an even more vital seaport: Baltimore, Maryland.

They approached Baltimore by land but were stalled when British General Robert Ross took a fatal gunshot to the chest by an American sharpshooter.

From the Atlantic waters, however, British warships began to surround Fort McHenry, the star-shaped fort that protected Baltimore's harbor. Great Britain knew that this fort was the key to taking the city of Baltimore. For more than 24 hours, the British bombarded American troops at Fort McHenry with bombs and rockets, giving them everything they had. Cannons and long guns shot more than 266,000 pounds of munitions in this short time, and the explosions were loud enough to be heard 100 miles away in Philadelphia. One of the artillery shells made a direct hit on a massive stockpile of gunpowder. With more than 250,000 pounds of explosive on hand, it should have decimated Fort McHenry and anyone in the surrounding area. But, the shell didn't explode. It lodged in the ground. America was stuck between a rock and a hard place, but God was giving them a way out.

The night sky was illuminated by cannon charge, and there was rarely a moment when the bay was not glowing from the barrage. Nearly eight miles away, aboard an English vessel, the British detained a local lawyer who was sent to negotiate a prisoner release. Unaware of the outcome, the lawyer eagerly awaited the sunrise and with it, news of Baltimore's fate. His name was Francis Scott Key.

Having witnessed the siege firsthand, Key's eyes peered toward Fort McHenry, shaken and fearful. But, by the dawn's early light, he could ever so faintly discern a giant American flag waving in the distance, giving proof that Fort McHenry still stood. The Americans weathered the British onslaught, stopping the British advancement, and "our flag was still there."

> The patriot who feels himself in service of God, who acknowledges Him in all his ways, has the promise of Almighty direction, and will find His word in his greatest darkness. —Francis Scott Key

More than 1,000 American troops held Fort McHenry, and miraculously, not one of them was brushed by enemy fire. The siege was a humiliating failure for Great Britain. Embarrassed and dumbstruck, British officers called for all of their ships to withdraw from the harbor.

Francis Scott Key, so moved by the sight of the American flag waving proudly in the distance, wrote a poem as a symbol of America's triumph and endurance.

> Then, in that hour of deliverance, my heart spoke. Does not such a country, and such defenders of their country, deserve a song? —Francis Scott Key

With a renewed sense of pride for his country, Key, still being held captive, furiously scribbled words on the back of a letter he had kept in his pocket. Originally entitled, "Defence of Fort M'Henry," these words would later come to be known as "The Star-Spangled Banner." With the help of his brother-in-law, Key set his poem to the tune of an old English tavern song.

As the years and the decades passed, so did the increasing popularity of the song. Bands played it during public events, namely July 4TH celebrations. In 1889, Secretary of the Navy Benjamin F. Tracy signed General Order #374, marking "The Star-Spangled Banner" as the official tune to be played during the raising of the American flag.

By the early 20TH century, there were various versions of the song in popular use. Seeking a singular, standard version, President Woodrow Wilson tasked the U.S. Bureau of Education

President Woodrow Wilson tasked the U.S. Bureau of Education with providing that official version. In response, the Bureau enlisted the help of five musicians to agree upon an arrangement. Those musicians were Walter Damrosch, Will Earhart, Arnold J. Gantvoort, Oscar Sonneck, and John Philip Sousa. The standardized version voted upon by these five musicians premiered at Carnegie Hall in New York City on December 5, 1917.

But, nearly 24 years passed before the United States officially adopted "The Star Spangled Banner" as its national anthem, signed by President Herbert Hoover on March 4, 1931.

Francis Scott Key continued writing poems, which primarily dealt with his love of country and his faith in God. Two of his more popular works, "Before the Lord We Bow" and "Lord, With Glowing Heart I'd Praise Thee," were used as Christian hymns. Writing from bed, he composed until his final days. The following was his final composition:

I have been a base and groveling thing
And now the dust of the earth my home,
But now I know that the end of my woe,
And the day of my bliss is come.
Then let them, like me, make ready their shrouds,
Nor shrink from the mortal strife,
And like me they shall sing, as to heaven they spring,
Death is not the end of life.

Expelled from Washington and thwarted at Baltimore, Great Britain's damaged fleet abandoned the Atlantic coastline. But, the War of 1812 was far from over. The fragile British fleet limped south to Jamaica to regroup, repair, and wait for reinforcements. If they couldn't take Baltimore, their next effort would be to seize New Orleans—an ambitious campaign that would cut American access to the Mississippi River, the lifeline of the West.

On November 16, 1814, President James Madison proclaimed a national day of public humiliation, fasting, and prayer.

> The two Houses of the National Legislature having by a joint resolution expressed their desire that in the present time of public calamity and war, a day may be recommended to be observed by the people of the United States as a day of public humiliation and fasting and of prayer to Almighty God for the safety and welfare of these States, His blessing on their arms, and a speedy restoration of peace ... Of confessing their sins and transgressions, and of strengthening their vows of repentance ... That He would be graciously pleased to pardon all their offenses ... I have deemed it proper to recommend a day of humble adoration to the Great Sovereign of the Universe. —James Madison

With winter approaching, the war was turning out to be tougher than either side expected. Even Great Britain began searching for a way to remove itself from combat and offered to negotiate directly with American diplomats. President Madison sent Henry Clay and John Quincy Adams to lead peace talks in the Belgian city of Ghent.

In the beginning, negotiations went nowhere. Every time the United States would make a proposal, Britain would refuse. With additional troops, commanders, and ships now available from the conclusion of the Napoleonic Wars, British military leaders felt it would only be a matter of time before they could gain the upper hand. The negotiations were simply a stalling tactic—stalling for that signature victory to turn the tide.

But, when news of more British retreats began to reach Ghent, Great Britain's resolve began to falter. Their will to fight was eroded further by the eagerness of British merchants to renew trade with America, and by the weariness of a tax-burdened English public that had been waiting nearly 20 years for their sons and husbands to return home from combat.

The question would quickly become, "Could a British military invasion of New Orleans outpace the negotiations in Ghent?" If New Orleans were taken, any treaty would be waived. Recently discovered documents from the National Archives in London instructed British General Pakenham directly, "If you hear of a peace treaty, pay no attention, continue to fight."

But, there was a breakthrough in negotiations. Great Britain finally decided that fighting the United States of America was not in their best interest. One by one, British demands were dropped, and American points were agreed to until representatives on both sides agreed to return prisoners and end the war.

On Christmas Eve, 1814, the Treaty of Ghent was signed. Once both countries ratified it, it would end the war, but news of the treaty traveled slowly across the Atlantic, and it would be weeks until it reached its destination. While American and

British diplomatic relations were on the mend, a showdown was already brewing in the Gulf of Mexico.

Unaware that peace had been reached under the Treaty of Ghent, events continued to unfold on the U.S. mainland. Anything that took place before the ratification of the treaty by both governments could be considered fair game, and the British already had their crosshairs set, with New Orleans as their prize.

With New Orleans essentially unprotected and the Royal Navy steadily making its way into the Gulf of Mexico, British victory in New Orleans seemed inevitable. The British fleet was more than 10,000 strong. The entire American army stood at less than 7,000, and they were spread thin across the country. With no great military commander or any significant military presence, New Orleans was all but lost.

America needed a leader; it needed a hero; it needed a Washington; it needed an answer that only Providence could provide. That answer came in the form of one of the greatest individual warriors, military strategists, and battlefield tacticians in U.S. history. He was the American Lion, Andrew Jackson.

It seemed like destiny for Andrew Jackson to face the British on the field of battle. His heart held a cold hatred for the redcoats dating back to his early years serving the American cause in the war for independence. During the Revolutionary War, a 13-year-old Jackson informally served as a courier to the local militia, but he and his brother were captured by British soldiers and held as prisoners for more than two years.

Their captors would often abuse and mistreat the boys for their own amusement. One night, a British officer ordered

Jackson to clean his muddy boots—the one's that were still on his feet. Jackson refused, and the officer slashed at him with his sword, leaving scars on both his hand and his forehead. Bloodied, cold, malnourished, and suffering from smallpox, Jackson still refused. His steadfast resolve in the face of pain, fear, and heartache would serve him well in the years to come.

Jackson's brother succumbed to smallpox only days after their release, and his mother, after nursing Jackson back to health, died trying to save his cousins, who were also afflicted with the disease. Having never met his father, who died just weeks before his birth, Andrew Jackson was left an orphan at the age of 15. A self-made man, Jackson would go on to become a lawyer, businessman, congressman, militia leader, and, finally, major general in the army.

In 1814, the newly minted Major General Andrew Jackson, his 968-man militia, and their Native American allies were fresh off a victory at Horseshoe Bend in Alabama where he had been fighting in the Creek Wars. Jackson's Cherokee allies played a crucial role in this decisive battle that claimed more than 800 of the 1,000 British soldiers who fought against them. Jackson only lost 50. This battle was integral to stopping the British as they had planned to take Mobile, followed by an invasion of New Orleans by land. When they were unable to gain their staging point in Mobile, the British quickly moved their navy to the Louisiana coastline.

President Madison and military top brass considered Jackson too brash and unpredictable. But, with no other viable options, he was their only choice to defend New Orleans. When Jackson received word of the British naval advancement toward New Orleans, he and his band of troops raced westward into New Orleans. Upon arrival, they found a city that was completely vulnerable, with no defensive positions and many entrance points. They would be fortunate to set up even the most rudimentary defense before a British invasion. Jackson and his men immediately got to work, shoring up American defenses along the Gulf Coast.

Jackson knew that he needed more men to put up a fight against what could be up to 10,000 of the most seasoned soldiers in the world. So, he began recruiting any and everyone he could find, employing any tactic he could think of to provide an edge to his outnumbered, outclassed, and inexperienced crew.

Jackson sent for experienced hunters and frontiersmen, using connections with some of his former men, like Davy Crocket, to call on the volunteers from Tennessee and dead-shot marksmen from Kentucky. Jackson also recruited pirates and privateers—men like Jean Lafitte—promising to look the other way on their past transgressions and pardoning their criminal smuggling charges in exchange for tactical help, boats, and experienced cannoneers to man their lines. He recruited a local businessman's sharpshooting club for snipers. He brought in women for constructing breastworks and maintaining supply lines. There were regiments of freedmen, Creoles, and Cajuns. He welcomed local volunteers and veterans of former Spanish and French occupations. His older Indian allies recruited local Choctaw warriors.

In all, General Jackson scraped together more than 4,000 of the most ragtag group of citizen soldiers ever assembled, and he was ready to put his motley crew to work.

Jackson declared martial law in New Orleans and put every ounce of time and energy into building the strongest possible defense. He set up his offices on Royal Street in the French Quarter, near what is now known as Jackson Square. His headquarters were in the shadows of Saint Louis Cathedral, where he implored sisters from the local convent to pray around the clock. Jackson was a Presbyterian, but he figured they needed all the help they could get.

Nicknamed "Old Hickory" for his legendary toughness, surviving countless duels, and with a bullet still lodged in his chest, Andrew Jackson was battling two chronic infections from wounds and a bout of dysentery as he prepared his men for battle. Local townsfolk were disheartened by his gaunt appearance, thinking, "How is this man going to save us when he looks like he's got one foot in the grave already?" Yet, despite his ailments, he welcomed the challenge. He was itching for a chance to confront the British, and the fire in his eyes dispelled his sickly visage. In a previous battle, he once wrote to his wife, "I owe to Britain a debt of retaliatory vengeance ... I trust I shall pay the debt."

Before Jackson could devise a practical plan for defending the city, the British anchored their ships near the mouth of the Mississippi River. Guarding the entry to the waterways leading into New Orleans were five American gunboats on Lake Borgne. But, 150 men and a mere 20 guns were no match for the 45 British barges manned by more than 1,200 men with an endless supply of ammunition. All the British had to do now was find a path through the swampy coast and onto dry land to stage their assault.

Jackson had his men to navigate the backwater bayous leading directly into New Orleans. They felled trees and collapsed small canals to block any direct path for the British. He fortified his flanks and redirected any possible British attack points to the Chalmette plantation, an open strip of land that had the mighty Mississippi on one side and swamps on the other. With the British approaching from the south, this would be Jackson's most ideal area to employ his tactical alignments.

Now that Jackson had set up a clearly defined battlefield, he could focus his reinforcement on one primary area. There was a drainage ditch that he expanded into a small canal, with breastworks and enforcements on the far side of the direction of attack. The fortification was several feet high, so an attack would require going down into the canal, climbing back up to ground level, and then up another five feet to get over the top of the fort. If they could finish in time, it would provide the best possible cover on such short notice.

Luckily, the British were having a tough time navigating the swamps, and all of the paths were obstructed. Well, all but one. The one path Jackson forgot about was the aptly named Bayou Bienvenue, ironically meaning "welcome" in French. The British found the path through the open bayou and unbeknownst to Jackson, they were already reaching the shore.

British forces followed their passage through Bayou Bienvenue and stormed ashore unopposed, immediately taking the Villere plantation. A local militia commander who lived on the plantation managed to escape and rushed to Jackson's camp to warn him that time was running out. When word reached

Jackson, he shouted, "By the eternal, they shall not sleep on our soil. I will smash them, so help me God!"

DECEMBER 23, 1814

With the unexpected advancement of the British, Jackson planned a daring night attack, taking advantage of the only tactical edge the Americans had at the time—the element of surprise.

British troops had expected very little resistance from the Americans, and many thought they would simply march into New Orleans unopposed, just as they had in Washington, D.C. After having no difficulty with the American gunboats on Lake Borgne and conquering the plantation without a soul in sight, these beliefs seemed unquestionable for the British. They relaxed. They built fires, cooked warm meals, and readied the camp to settle in for the night. Then, the American artillery started to fall.

Jackson sent a 14-gun schooner downriver alongside the camp to bombard British positions. He instructed his men to simply aim for the fires. At the same time, General Jackson silently advanced southward with mobile artillery and his best 2,000 men, stopping just outside the British camp.

When the schooner's barrage began, Jackson and his men opened up with artillery from the ground. British officers quickly extinguished the fires, leaving the battlefield pitch black, but the Americans had already pinpointed their positions. With visibility limited to the flashes of gunfire, Jackson ordered his soldiers to charge the redcoats. The battle quickly went hand-to-hand and bayonet-to-bayonet. It wasn't long, however, before it became impossible to know which way to fire or where the battle lines were, so Jackson called for his men to fall back.

General Jackson's ragtag army held their own against the world's greatest military power, standing toe-to-toe with them on the battlefield. There were roughly an even number of casualties on each side, yet this only emboldened the American force. It gave them invaluable experience fighting together and generated an even greater sense of urgency to complete fortifications now that the threat was at their doorstep.

For Great Britain, this was a giant red flag. For them, it was now apparent this would not be the cakewalk they were expecting, and it gave the British officers pause in making further troop movements. Instead, they decided to wait for additional supplies and reinforcement. In retrospect, this decision would prove to be crucial. Many historians believe that had the British continued to advance, they may have likely taken New Orleans.

The lull in action allowed Jackson to further prepare his fortifications, but it also granted the British plenty of time to draw in more troops along with their battlefield commander, General Sir Edward Pakenham. A respected leader, General Pakenham was appointed as commander of British forces, and while his men were happy to see him arrive, Pakenham wasn't pleased with the lack of British progress along the Gulf Coast. With his command structure now in place, however, they were freshly reinforced, re-supplied, and re-energized.

JANUARY 1, 1815

With Pakenham's army now over 8,000 strong and fielding its full array of artillery, he ordered his men to attack American positions and weaken their fortifications. This quickly escalated into a three-hour artillery exchange with Jackson's surprisingly precise cannons. Just as the British were beginning to gain ground, Pakenham was forced to call for retreat. They had run out of ammunition.

The British fell back to their camp and waited for additional munitions, which were taking much longer than expected. The supply lines ran through 60 miles of heavy swamps and thick mud. Any supplies coming in had to be carried in rowboats and then dragged across miles of muddy fields. Pakenham was, again, forced to wait. In the interim, he requested to change their battle plan, wishing to attack from a more favorable position, but British Admiral Sir Alexander Cochrane dismissed his request outright. Cochrane still felt that the untrained, undersupplied, and undisciplined American line of "backwoods rabble" would collapse against the British advance, saying, "If you can't defeat the Americans with your army, I'll do so with my sailors."

General Pakenham was now forced, against his better judgment, to play the cards he was dealt. Morale among his men was declining each day with abnormally frigid temperatures, back-breaking supply runs, and dashed expectations of a quick and easy occupation. They were also suffering guerrilla-style assaults from snipers and almost nightly sneak attacks led in small parties by Jackson's elite Native warriors. With the situation unlikely to improve in the near-term, Pakenham decided that as soon as his artillery was fully restocked, he would attack with full force.

One week later, the stage was set. There were to be no more dress rehearsals, no more reconnaissance expeditions or artillery probes. The British were finally ready to attack, full volume.

The gravity of the situation at hand became clear to Jackson. He knew what he was up against, and he knew that he and his men might soon face their fate. Alone, in silent reflection the night before battle, Jackson penned a letter to his wife, Rachel:

> My love, I am fearful this might be the end for our young nation. America has met its match in the British, yet again, but this time it may be too much. I assure you, however, we will not give up without a fight. The brave must face the enemy. Should it be the will of divine providence, I will see you before long. I shall return to your arms on the wings of love and affection. Until then, my dearest heart, summon up your resolution and bear my absence with fortitude. Tell little Andrew that his papa will be home shortly, and that he sends him three sweet kisses. Affectionately Yours, Andrew.

JANUARY 8, 1815, 5 A.M.

Pakenham devised an ambitious plan with multiple moving parts. It would require efficient movement and good timing, but if executed properly, it would be nearly unstoppable. British efficiency and strategy defeated Napoleon. Why would the Americans prove any different?

The battle began that morning with perfect conditions for General Pakenham and his multi-front plan of attack. The plains of Chalmette were blanketed in a thick fog that would cover their troop movements on the field, but the sight lines were still clear downriver to observe the timing of the movements and progress of the mission at hand.

On the American side, there was nervous apprehension as the experienced band of battle-hardened British soldiers advanced under the cover of a heavy fog. The advantage of Jackson's precise marksmen and accurate cannons were of little use without clear targets. Running low on firearms, many of the volunteers held in reserve were equipped with farm tools, knives, and melee weapons. Raw, patched together, and standing behind a fortress jerry-rigged with cotton bales and sugar barrels, the Americans were fighting for a piece of land that wasn't even a part of their country a decade before. But, it was their duty. It was their mission. It was their home. And they were all that stood between freedom and captivity.

> Here, we shall plant our stakes! And not abandon them until we drive these redcoat rascals into the river, or the swamp. —Andrew Jackson

The flare of Congreve rockets whistled overhead, signaling the start of the British advance. Organized and solidified columns of red-coated soldiers let out a cheer and began their march toward the American line.

As the drumbeats grew louder and the rhythmic vibrations of marching soldiers and artillery blasts shook the earth, providence was about to provide the Americans a path to victory.

Just as the clockwork machinations of Pakenham's plan began to unfold, the thick fog suddenly vanished from the field. It rolled down along the riverbanks, blanketing the river from shore to shore, exposing the slow moving formations of the British attack columns, and giving Jackson a clear idea of Pakenham's strategy. The tables had turned. With their long rifles, Jackson's sharpshooters were able to pinpoint their targets with brilliant accuracy, and they knew exactly who to aim for—the officers on horseback. They opened fire.

The fog also clouded the sight lines of Pakenham's view of the river, and he lost track of the progress of his secondary assault. He wouldn't have been happy with what he saw anyway. The canal they used to move their boats had partially collapsed from American artillery fire. The boats had to be dragged to shore, and they got mired on the muddy banks, delaying their launch. With the fog now on the river, they were unable to see their landing positions on the far side, and with an unusually strong current, they were miles further downstream when they finally crossed, entirely out of position for an immediate attack.

Back on the main battlefield, British troops continued their approach toward the American fortification. An officer shouted for scaling ladders, but none appeared. The ladders had been mistakenly left back at their camp. Without scaling equipment, they had no way to attack the fortifications. They were sitting ducks. The officer panicked and sent part of his unit back to their camp for the ladders. The rest of them started taking on fire. A nearby British general, confused by the troops running back to camp, crossed the field and saw the problem. He promised the failed officer that he would see him hanged. But, the irate general would never get the opportunity. An American sniper got to him first.

The short-range cannons were filled with "grapeshot," ammunition that consisted of tiny steel balls. When they were all fired at once, it was like that of a giant shotgun blast. These grapeshots were turning redcoats into a red mist.

By this time, the Americans had killed so many British officers that none of the troops knew what to do. Wait for the ladders? Retreat to safety? Stand in formation? Amid the confusion, some of them marched directly into a wall of guns and cannon fire. Others stood at attention, awaiting orders.

American gunmen poured it on, crushing the front lines as they advanced. In a matter of minutes, the majority of British officers was dead. Before the end of the hour, two generals, six majors, eight colonels, 22 captains, and 54 junior officers also met their fate.

General Andrew Jackson watched the hail of destruction from a perch behind the fortification. It became clear to Jackson that Pakenham had counted too heavily on moving under the cover of a thick morning fog.

> Give it to 'em, boys! Let us finish this business today!
> —Andrew Jackson

Old Hickory's militiamen fired their guns with punishing precision. British soldiers fell in waves. With most of their leaders dead or wounded, hundreds of frantic redcoats were now trying to make a run for it, only to be devastated by a hail of musket balls.

The British unit that rushed back to camp to retrieve the ladders finally arrived on the scene, but they were too late. Some were able to climb the fortification, but there were now too few to make any difference, and they were picked off one by one.

Pakenham was stunned by the speed at which his men were falling. His brilliant plan not only unraveled, it collapsed. He could hold back no longer. Pakenham took it upon himself to lead a desperate charge to the front. His formation was immediately riddled by rifle and cannon fire. Seconds later, Pakenham caught a blast of grapeshot and was killed.

With Pakenham eliminated and the majority of his officers out of commission, the British plan of attack descended into utter chaos. Red-coated soldiers were now retreating in droves. A few valiant troops, lacking any direction from officers, tried to climb the wall by hand, only to founder with each frantic grasp. Finally, the full retreat was sounded. In a battle that lasted no more than 30 minutes, the British were annihilated.

That morning, Pakenham's brave and disciplined redcoats ran into a murderous hail of artillery shells and rifle fire. One of his regiments, the Scottish Highlanders, were so disciplined that it actually led to their undoing. With their commanding officers killed or out of position, they could not advance without an order, but they would also refuse to retreat without one either. They held their ground. As the first men on their lines were killed, the men behind would move forward to hold their position. They dropped like flies. Andrew Jackson would later say it looked like an unmoving brick wall with more men constantly moving forward and taking fire.

With the sunrise, the fog lifted, but now the smoke was so thick from artillery and cannon fire, one could hardly tell the difference. When the smoke finally cleared, it looked at first glance like a sea of blood; only it wasn't blood. The red-coated uniforms of the British Army were scattered on the horizon, the field entirely covered with lifeless bodies. In parts, they were lying in piles of three or four, one on top of the other.

> Within a few hundred yards were nearly a thousand bodies, all of them in British uniforms. Not a single American was among them. They were thrown by dozens into shallow holes, scarcely deep enough to furnish them with a slight covering of earth. An American officer stood by smoking a cigar, and apparently counting the slain with a look of savage exultation, and repeating over and over to each individual that approached him, that their loss amounted only to seven men killed and six wounded. —British officer captured by U.S. troops.

The War of 1812 is still a relatively forgotten war in American history. Many will claim that victory in New Orleans didn't matter, citing the war was over when the Treaty of Ghent was signed. Yet, some may argue that it was the most important war of them all. After all, what if the U.S. had lost the Battle of New Orleans? The treaty had yet to be ratified, and the British might have exploited the possession of New Orleans had they won control of the city. So, actually, it wasn't fought for nothing. In fact, it meant everything to the future of the United States. Captain Henry Garland of the volunteer cavalry said it best: "Most people say that our republic was born on the fourth day of July, 1776, at Philadelphia. This is not true. It was only begotten then. It was born when Cornwallis yielded at Yorktown. But, it was never confirmed until the 8th of January, 1815."

British forces had mounted a full-scale attack on New Orleans, only to be met with a sound defeat at the hands of General Andrew Jackson and his ragtag army. Nearly 5,000 British troops had either been wounded or killed. As one British officer put it, "There never was a more complete failure."

Jackson addressed his troops shortly after the battle, boasting about his group of mismatched misfits who were able to come together, despite their differences in background, abilities, and experience, for a common cause of protecting their homes, their freedom, and their country.

> Natives of different states, acting together, for the first time in this camp ... Have reaped the fruits of an honorable union.
> —Andrew Jackson

Like a Louisiana gumbo, Jackson had taken the unique and mismatched ingredients of society and blended them together in the proverbial melting pot. In coming together, they didn't just become more; they became better. Like the Latin creed on American currency that reads "E Pluribus Unum," meaning "out of many, one," this group came together and grew through adversity, forging a common bond among them. No longer did their labels, limitations, or differences define them. They were something better now. As one united nation, under God, they were indivisible. Together, they were Americans.

Two weeks after the war ended, President James Madison proclaimed a National Day of Thanksgiving, acknowledging Almighty God for His providential hand on America and victory in battle. General Jackson shared the same sentiment. For him, success was unattainable without the providential hand of God:

> It appears that the unerring hand of Providence shielded my men from the shower of balls, bombs, and rockets, when every ball and bomb from our guns carried with them a mission of death. Heaven, to be sure, has interposed most wonderfully in our behalf, and I am filled with gratitude when I look back to what we have escaped. —Andrew Jackson

Old Hickory would ride the wave of his newfound celebrity into politics and all the way to the White House, eventually serving as America's seventh president. Years later, on his death bed, Jackson wrote of his belief in the American people and of his faith in Christ.

> Americans are not a perfect people, but we are called to a perfect mission. Providence has showered on this favored

> land blessings without number, and has chosen you as the guardians of freedom, to preserve it for the benefit of the human race. May He who holds in His hands the destinies of nations make you worthy of the favors He has bestowed, and enable you, with pure hearts and hands and sleepless vigilance, to guard and defend to the end of time, the great charge He has committed to your keeping. Do not weep for me; I am in the hands of a merciful God. I have full confidence in his goodness and mercy. The Bible, the rock upon which our republic rests, is true. Upon that sacred volume I rest my hope for eternal salvation, through the merits and blood of our blessed Lord and Savior, Jesus Christ. —Andrew Jackson

At Jackson's funeral, Massachusetts Governor Benjamin F. Butler called him "some heaven-appointed and heaven-assisted warrior." And of his leadership in New Orleans, "Who in these things does not see the hand of God?"

Amid the jubilation and renewed sense of patriotism that followed the War of 1812, Americans began to transform their young nation as it grew in size, population, and power. Hundreds of thousands of people streamed westward, ushering in the so-called "Era of Good Feelings," fostering the notion that American expansion was its "manifest destiny." It boosted the confidence of a nation and encouraged the growing spirit of American ideals.

At the same time, the war also launched the U.S. toward economic independence, as the interruption of trade with Europe had encouraged the growth of American manufactures. Finally, after 40 years of independence, it dawned on the world that the new American republic might be emerging as a world power.

The United States of America had survived a "second war of independence" against the greatest military power on earth. It was an important turning point—a watershed moment in American history—having a far-reaching impact on the growth of a maturing republic. With it emerged new symbols of nationhood, a new gallery of heroes, and a reinvigorated idea of what it was to be an American. It established the credibility of a young nation among other nations. It declared to the world that America was here to stay; that it was not just some grand experiment, but the ultimate testament to a nation founded on the Word of God through a personal relationship with Jesus Christ.

REFERENCES

Barton, David. *Original Intent: The Courts, the Constitution & Religion*. WallBuilder Press. 2000.

Barton, David. *The Founders' Bible*. Edited by Brad Cummings and Lance Wubbels. Shiloh Road Publishers. 2014.

Beliles, Mark A., and Stephen K. McDowell. *America's Providential History*. The Providence Foundation. 1989.

Booty, John E. *The Church in History*. Morehouse Publishing. 2003.

Dreisbach, Daniel L., and Mark David Hall, eds. *The Sacred Rights of Conscience.* Liberty Fund Inc. 2009.

Dreisbach, Daniel L., and Mark David Hall, eds. *Faith and the Founders of the American Republic.* Oxford University Press. 2014.

Federer, Susie. *Miracles in American History: 32 Amazing Stories of Answered Prayer*. Amerisearch Inc. 2012.

Federer, William J. *America's God and Country*. Amerisearch Inc. 2011.

Federer, William J. *Change to Chains.* Amerisearch Inc. 2011.

Federer, William J. *American Minute*. Amerisearch Inc. 2012.

Gaustad, Edwin S. *Faith of Our Fathers: Religion and the New Nation*. Harpercollins. 1987.

Hutchins, Robert Maynard, ed. *Great Books of the Western World-Encyclopedia Britannica*. Encyclopedia Britannica.
Vol. 35: Locke/Berkeley/Hume. 1986.
Vol. 38: Montesquieu/Rousseau. 1984

Manuel, David, and Peter Marshall. *The Light and the Glory*. Revell. 2009.

Marshall, Peter. *Restoring America*. Peter Marshall Ministries. 2007.

Swaggart, Jimmy. *The Expositor's Study Bible*. Jimmy Swaggart Ministries. 2005.

Wilson, Woodrow. *A History of the American People*. HardPress Publishing. 2013.